Pre-Algebra and Algebra Warm-ups

Authors: Cindy Barden and Wendi Silvano
Editor: Mary Dieterich
Proofreaders: April Albert and Margaret Brown

COPYRIGHT © 2016 Mark Twain Media, Inc.

ISBN 978-1-62223-586-5

Printing No. CD-404241

Mark Twain Media, Inc., Publishers
Distributed by Carson-Dellosa Publishing LLC

The purchase of this book entitles the buyer to reproduce the student pages for classroom use only. Other permissions may be obtained by writing Mark Twain Media, Inc., Publishers.

All rights reserved. Printed in the United States of America.

Table of Contents

Introduction

The *Pre-Algebra and Algebra Warm-Ups* book provides students with a daily dose of math activities to get them warmed up for a day's lesson or to review what has already been learned. It is important for students to review and practice the skills they gain as they learn pre-algebra and algebra. Revisiting math skills several days after they are first learned is a helpful way to reinforce those skills.

The short warm-up activities presented in this book provide teachers and parents with activities to help students practice and reinforce the skills they have already learned. They are encouraged to use a variety of problem-solving techniques, including making lists, logical reasoning, using and drawing diagrams, and using tables to find patterns. Students may need to complete some of the activities on their own paper.

Topics covered in *Pre-Algebra and Algebra Warm-Ups* include basic concepts such as math operations, fractions, decimals, and integers. Topics progress to exponents, factors, equations, and graphing. More advanced concepts include polynomials, probability, rational expressions, square roots and radicals, and quadratic equations. Activities become progressively more challenging as the book goes on, but they can be used in any order to best meet your teaching needs.

Each page may be copied and cut apart so that the individual sections can be used as quick warm-up activities to begin each day. The teacher may also give the student the entire page to keep in a folder or binder and complete as assigned. A transparency of the page may be made to project the activities for the whole class to see. A digital copy of the page can also be projected on the class whiteboard or projection device.

Extra copies of warm-ups may also be kept in the class learning center for students to complete when they have spare time for review or when the class has a few minutes before lunch or dismissal.

Pre-Algebra and Algebra Warm-Ups supports the NCTM standards for mathematics. Also, the book has been correlated to current state, national, and provincial standards. Correlations for the book that apply to your location and needs may be found at www.carsondellosa.com.

Name: _____   Date: _____

Pre-Algebra

#001. Addition and the Value of *n*

Find the value of *n*.

A. $5 + n = 16$ $n =$ _____

B. $7 + n = 16$ $n =$ _____

C. $6 + n = 20$ $n =$ _____

D. $9 + n = 18$ $n =$ _____

#002. Addition and the Value of *p*

Find the value of *p*.

A. $p + \$17 = \$35$ $p =$ _____

B. $\$21 + p = \$47$ $p =$ _____

C. $p + \$34 = \$48$ $p =$ _____

D. $\$11 + p = \$50$ $p =$ _____

#003. Addition and the Value of *h*

Write the value of *h*.

A. $0.42 + h = 0.86$ $h =$ _____

B. $h + 0.74 = 0.92$ $h =$ _____

C. $0.61 + h = 0.73$ $h =$ _____

D. $h + 0.49 = 0.91$ $h =$ _____

#004. Addition and the Value of *t*

Find the value of *t*.

A. $7 + t + 4 = 19$ $t =$ _____

B. $12 + t + 5 = 23$ $t =$ _____

C. $t + 8 + 4 = 31$ $t =$ _____

D. $14 + 6 + t = 25$ $t =$ _____

Name: _____   Date: _____

Pre-Algebra

#005. Subtraction and the Value of *n*

Find the value of *n*.

A. $45 - n = 35$ $n =$ _____

B. $27 - n = 16$ $n =$ _____

C. $66 - n = 20$ $n =$ _____

D. $91 - n = 18$ $n =$ _____

#006. Subtraction and the Value of *p*

Find the value of *p*.

A. $p - \$17 = \$35$ $p =$ _____

B. $\$91 - p = \$47$ $p =$ _____

C. $p - \$34 = \$48$ $p =$ _____

D. $\$89 - p = \$50$ $p =$ _____

#007. Subtraction and the Value of *h*

Write the value of *h*.

A. $h - 0.42 = 0.87$ $h =$ _____

B. $h - 0.74 = 0.92$ $h =$ _____

C. $0.61 - h = 0.33$ $h =$ _____

D. $h - 0.49 = 0.91$ $h =$ _____

#008. Subtraction and the Value of *t*

Find the value of *t*.

A. $7 - t + 14 = 19$ $t =$ _____

B. $12 - t + 25 = 23$ $t =$ _____

C. $t - 8 - 4 = 31$ $t =$ _____

D. $74 - 6 - t = 25$ $t =$ _____

Name: _____ Date: _____

Pre-Algebra

#009. Multiplication and the Value of *m*

Find the value of *m*.

A. $5 \times m = 25$ $m =$ _____

B. $4 \times m = 16$ $m =$ _____

C. $m \times 3 = 21$ $m =$ _____

D. $m \times 7 = 42$ $m =$ _____

#010. Multiplication and the Value of *p*

Find the value of *p*.

A. $25 \times p = 100$ $p =$ _____

B. $41 \times p = 123$ $p =$ _____

C. $15 \times p = 105$ $p =$ _____

D. $p \times 4 = 24$ $p =$ _____

#011. Multiplication and the Value of *k*

Write the value of *k*.

A. $3 \times 5 \times k = 30$ $k =$ _____

B. $k \times 7 \times 2 = 56$ $k =$ _____

C. $4 \times k \times 3 = 36$ $k =$ _____

D. $k \times 4 \times 9 = 108$ $k =$ _____

#012. Multiplication and the Value of *s*

Find the value of *s*.

A. $s^2 = 100$ $s =$ _____

B. $40 \times s = 160$ $s =$ _____

C. $11 \times s = 99$ $s =$ _____

D. $8 \times s = 56$ $s =$ _____

Name: _____ Date: _____

Pre-Algebra

#013. Division and the Value of w

Find the value of w.

A. $36 \div w = 6$ $w =$ _____

B. $w \div 8 = 6$ $w =$ _____

C. $99 \div w = 9$ $w =$ _____

D. $w \div 7 = 5$ $w =$ _____

#014. Division and the Value of v

Find the value of v.

A. $\$55 \div v = \$11$ $v =$ _____

B. $v \div 14 = \$3$ $v =$ _____

C. $\$81 \div v = \$9$ $v =$ _____

D. $v \div 12 = \$11$ $v =$ _____

#015. Division and the Value of r

Find the value of r. Remember to include the remainder when you are looking for the answer.

A. $45 \div r = 7 \text{ R}3$ $r =$ _____

B. $r \div 8 = 7 \text{ R}2$ $r =$ _____

C. $86 \div r = 9 \text{ R}5$ $r =$ _____

D. $r \div 11 = 5 \text{ R}9$ $r =$ _____

#016. Division and the Value of h

Find the value of h.

A. $1{,}000 \div h = 100$ $h =$ _____

B. $h \div 5 = 20$ $h =$ _____

C. $100{,}000 \div h = 100$ $h =$ _____

D. $h \div 30 = 2{,}100$ $h =$ _____

Name: _____ Date: _____

Pre-Algebra

#017. Mixed Operations: Math Stories 1

A. Grandma baked cookies. She gave 7 to Sandy. She gave half of what were left, plus one, to Sue. She gave 3 to Stan. Then she gave half of what were left to Steve. Since there were only two cookies left, she ate them herself. How many cookies did she bake?

_____

B. In a game, each player receives the same amount of play money. They each get twenty-five $1's, three $5's, four $10's, two $100's. How much money does each player get?

_____

C. Jacob had 7 dimes, 14 nickels, 3 quarters, and 2 half-dollars. How much money did he have in all?

_____

#018. Mixed Operations: Math Stories 2

A. Juan has fewer than ten $10 bills. He has more than three $1 bills. He has twice as many tens as ones. How much money does he have?

_____

B. At a farmer's market, carrots are on sale, three bunches for $1. Each bunch contains five carrots. How many carrots would you get for $3?

_____

#019. Writing Decimals as Fractions

Write the **decimals** as **fractions**. Reduce to lowest terms.

A. $0.75 =$ _____ **B.** $0.95 =$ _____

C. $0.2 =$ _____ **D.** $0.34 =$ _____

E. $0.01 =$ _____ **F.** $7.14 =$ _____

#020. Writing Fractions as Decimals

Write the **fractions** as **decimals**.

A. $\frac{4}{5} =$ _____ **B.** $\frac{9}{10} =$ _____

C. $\frac{7}{100} =$ _____ **D.** $\frac{7}{8} =$ _____

E. $\frac{2}{4} =$ _____ **F.** $5\frac{3}{5} =$ _____

Name: _____   Date: _____

Pre-Algebra

#021. Decimals and Fractions: Missing Numbers 1

Fill in the missing numbers to make the equations true. Reduce fractions to lowest terms.

A. $9\frac{1}{2} + 7\frac{3}{4} = $ _____

B. $3\frac{5}{8} - 2\frac{9}{10} = $ _____

C. $\frac{2}{3} \div \frac{9}{16} = $ _____

D. $\frac{4}{7} \times \frac{5}{8} = $ _____

#022. Decimals and Fractions: Missing Numbers 2

Fill in the missing numbers to make the equations true.

A. $\frac{3}{4} + $ _____ $= 1\frac{1}{4}$

B. $0.3 \times$ _____ $= 0.9$

C. $0.42 -$ _____ $= 0.24$

D. _____ $\div \frac{1}{2} = 10$

#023. Order of Operations

Review the **order of operations** steps. Solve the equations.

A. $3 \times 5 + 7 = $ _____

B. $6 + 2 \times 4 = $ _____

C. $5 + 3 \times 2 + 4 = $ _____

D. $11 + 7 + 4 \times 8 = $ _____

E. $5 \times 7 - 4 = $ _____

F. $11 \times 4 - 9 = $ _____

G. $8 - 3 \times 9 - 6 = $ _____

H. $13 - 5 - 2 \times 13 = $ _____

#024. Reviewing Order of Operations

Review the **order of operations** steps. Solve the equations.

A. $(6 + 2) \times (3 + 4) = $ _____

B. $(37 - 2) \div 7 = $ _____

C. $(9 \div 3) \times (2 \times 4) = $ _____

D. $(0.7 \times 0.2) - (0.5 + 0.3) = $ _____

E. $10^2 + 2 = $ _____

F. $(6 \times 3) \div (9 - 6) = $ _____

G. $3 \times 3^2 - 1 = $ _____

H. $(10 \div 2) + (24 - 12) \times (3 + 6) = $ _____

Name: _____   Date: _____

Pre-Algebra

#025. Positive and Negative Numbers

A. The temperature started at -8°.
It increased 19°.
The temperature is now _____.

B. The temperature started at 28°.
It decreased 19°.
The temperature is now _____.

C. The temperature started at -32°.
It increased 9°.
The temperature is now _____.

D. The temperature started at -17°.
It decreased 29°.
The temperature is now _____.

#026. Positive and Negative Numbers: Fill in the Blank 1

Use each of the following numbers only once in each equation to make each equation true.

-1, -3, and -5

A. _____ + _____ + _____ = -9

B. (_____ × _____) + _____ = +2

C. (_____ × _____) + _____ = +14

D. (_____ + _____) ÷ _____ = +8

#027. Positive and Negative Numbers: Fill in the Blank 2

Use each of the following numbers only once in each equation to make each equation true.

-5, -6, and -7

A. _____ + _____ + _____ = -18

B. (_____ × _____) + _____ = +37

C. (_____ × _____) + _____ = +23

D. (_____ × _____) ÷ _____ = 4 R2

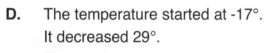
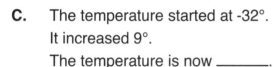
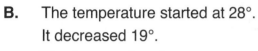

#028. Positive and Negative Numbers: Fill in the Blank 3

Use each of the following numbers only once in each equation to make each equation true.

-4, -5, -6

A. (_____ × _____) ÷ _____ = -7 R2

B. (_____ × _____) ÷ _____ = -4 R4

C. _____ + _____ + _____ = -15

D. _____ × (_____ + _____) = +54

Name: _____ Date: _____

Pre-Algebra

#029. Exponents

2^2 contains an **exponent**. It means the same as 2×2. The value of $2^2 = 4$.

2^3 contains an exponent. It means the same as $2 \times 2 \times 2$. The value of $2^3 = 8$.

A. 2^4 means the same as

_____.

B. 9^6 means the same as

_____.

C. 7^3 means the same as

_____.

D. y^{10} means the same as

_____.

#030. Exponential Expressions

Find the value of each **exponential expression**.

A. 3^3 _____   **B.** 4^2 _____

C. 2^5 _____   **D.** 5^3 _____

Write the exponential expression for each multiplication expression.

E. $3 \times 3 \times 3 =$ _____

F. $10 \times 10 \times 10 \times 10 \times 10 \times 10 =$ _____

G. $d \cdot d \cdot d =$ _____

H. $m \cdot m + p \cdot p =$ _____

#031. Solving for Exponents

Solve the equations.

A. $7 + 3^2 =$ _____

B. $42 - 4^2 =$ _____

C. $3^3 - 3 =$ _____

D. $9^2 - 48 =$ _____

Write the **exponential expressions** that equal the amounts given.

E. $36 =$ _____   **F.** $81 =$ _____

G. $16 =$ _____   **H.** $25 =$ _____

#032. Solving Multi-Step Math Stories

A. The Lovely Lawn Landscaping Company charges $8 per square foot to lay sod. Mr. Berenz needs new sod in an area 40 feet by 30 feet. How much will it cost him to have new sod laid? _____

B. The Lovely Lawn Landscaping Company charges 5¢ a pound for decorative rock, plus a $25 delivery fee. How much will it cost to have 3 tons of rock delivered?

_____

C. Mr. Mikkelson's six children bought their dad a new electric saw for Father's Day. His youngest daughter could only afford to contribute $20. The other five divided the rest of the cost equally among them. If the saw cost $170, how much did it cost each of the other children?

_____

Name: _____   Date: _____

Pre-Algebra

#033. Operations Signs: <, >, =

Write <, >, or = to make the number sentences true.

A.   17 _____ 2 × 7

B. n _____ $n + 8$

C. $n - 9$ _____ $n - 11$

D. $n + 14$ _____ $n + 7 + 7$

#034. Operations Signs: <, >, ≤, ≥, and =

Write <, >, ≤, ≥, or = to make the number sentences true.

A. $m + n + y + z$ _____ $n + m + z + y$

B. $t + u$ _____ $t - u$

C. $7v + 8v - 11v$ _____ $8v - 11v + 7v$

D. $6 × 4$ _____ $n + 2$, if $n = 9$

E. $16t$ _____ 32, if $t > 1$ and t is a whole number

F. $16t ÷ 2$ _____ $16t × 2$

G. $4 - z$ _____ 4, if $z ≥ 0$

#035. Mixed Operations 1

Work clockwise, starting at the top of the figure. Fill in the missing number. Your starting number is also your ending number.

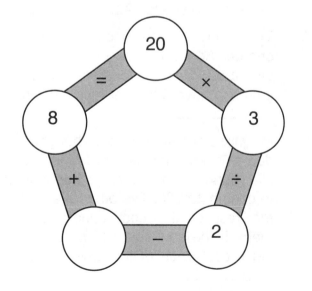

#036. Mixed Operations 2

Work clockwise, starting at the top of the figure. Fill in the missing number. Your starting number is also your ending number.

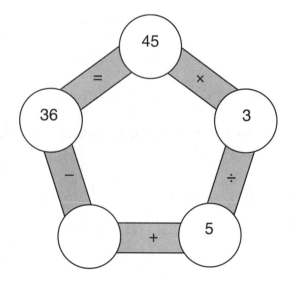

Name: _____   Date: _____

Pre-Algebra

#037. Describing Number Patterns

Find the **pattern**. Fill in the missing numbers. Describe the pattern **rule**.

A.   3, 7, 15, ____, 63, 127

Algebraic expression:

_____

B.   128, 64, 32, ____, 8, 4

Algebraic expression:

_____

C.   99, 88, ____, ____, ____, ____, 33

Algebraic expression:

_____

#038. Using Expressions to Describe Number Patterns

Write an algebraic expression to describe the **pattern**.

A.   One cat has two ears. Two cats have four ears. How many ears do an unknown number of cats have?

Algebraic expression:

_____

B.   Jason jogged three miles on Sunday and then jogged two more miles each day for a week.

Algebraic expression:

_____

#039. Drawing a Picture or Diagram

Drawing a picture or diagram can help you find patterns. The drawings do not need to be detailed. Use circles, X's, or squares to represent items from the problems below. Answer the questions on the lines provided.

A.   A mother duck led a large group of ducklings. There were two ducklings in the row behind her, and three ducklings in the row following them. All the ducklings followed the same pattern. There were five rows of ducklings. How many ducklings were there in all? On your own paper, draw a picture or diagram to represent the ducklings.

_____

B.   George stacked cans of tomato juice for a grocery store display. When he finished, (counting from the top down) there was one can on the top, two cans in the second layer, and six cans in the fourth layer. All layers except the top layer had an even number of cans. If he stacked all cans in this pattern, and the stack was six layers high, how many cans were in the bottom layer? On your own paper, draw a picture to show the story.

_____

Name: _____   Date: _____

Pre-Algebra

#040. Drawing a Diagram

Draw the next set of items in each pattern.

A.

B.

#041. Drawing a Picture

Draw a pattern of items for this algebraic expression: $n + 3$. Start with three items.

#042. Using Tables to Find Patterns

A. One cold January day, the temperature started dropping at 3 P.M. It dropped two degrees each hour until 10 P.M. Fill in the **table**.

If it was 3° at 3 P.M., what was the temperature at 10 P.M.? _____

Time	3 P.M.	4 P.M.	5 P.M.	6 P.M.	7 P.M.	8 P.M.	9 P.M.	10 P.M.
Temperature	3°	1°	___	___	___	___	___	___

B. Everett had 35 red and white balloons. He had two red ones for every three white ones. Fill in the table to find how many red ones he had.

How many were red? _____

red	2	4	___	___	___	___	___
white	3	6	___	___	___	___	___
total	5	10	___	___	___	___	___

Name: _____ Date: _____

Pre-Algebra

#043. Values of Variables 1

Find the value of the expression $47 + n$ when:

A. $n = 5$ _____

B. $n = 13$ _____

C. $n = 6$ _____

D. $n = 52$ _____

#044. Values of Variables 2

Find the value of the expression $71 - p$ when:

A. $p = 14$ _____

B. $p = 71$ _____

C. $p = 84$ _____

D. $p = 11$ _____

#045. Values of Variables 3

Find the value of the expression $40 - (m \times 4)$ when:

A. $m = 20$ _____

B. $m = 7$ _____

C. $m = 31$ _____

D. $m = 19$ _____

#046. Solving Word Problems With Values of Variables

A. A florist pays Mona 75¢ a bunch for dried lavender. Write an expression to show how much the florist will pay Mona for an unknown quantity of lavender. Let b equal the number of bunches Mona will sell.

_____

B. If Mona brings in 17 bunches of lavender, how much will the florist pay her?

_____

Name: _____ Date: _____

Pre-Algebra

#047. Balancing Equations With Addition

If the same amount is added to both sides of a **true equation**, the equation remains true.

Example: 3 + 4 = 7 is a true equation. If 5 is added to both sides, the new equation is also true: 3 + 4 + 5 = 7 + 5

Fill in the blanks to make the equations true.

A. 4 + 6 = 10

4 + 6 + _____ = 10 + 9

B. z + 3 = 6

z + 3 + 3 = 6 + _____

C. 17 − 11 = 6

17 − 11 + 12 = _____

#048. Balancing Equations With Subtraction

If the same amount is subtracted from both sides of a **true equation**, the equation remains true. Fill in the blanks to make the equations true.

Example: 11 − 4 = 7 is a true equation. If 5 is subtracted from both sides, the new equation is also true: 11 − 4 − 5 = 7 − 5

A. 16 − 9 = 7

16 − 9 − 5 = 7 − _____

B. 4 × 8 = 32

4 × 8 − _____ = 32 − 5

C. z + 9 = 31

z + 9 − 8 = _____

#049. Balancing Equations With Multiplication

If both sides of a **true equation** are multiplied by the same amount, the equation remains true. Fill in the blanks to make the equations true.

Example: 11 × 4 = 44 is a true equation. If 2 is multiplied on both sides, the new equation is also true: 11 × 4 × 2 = 44 × 2

A. 11 × 4 = 44

_____ × 11 + 4 = _____ × 44

B. z − 101 = 700

z − 101 × 4 = 700 × _____

C. z × 3 × 0.5 = 3

_____ = 6 × 3

#050. Balancing Equations With Division

If both sides of a **true equation** are divided by the same amount, the equation remains true. Fill in the blanks to make the equations true.

Example: 44 ÷ 11 = 4 is a true equation. If 2 is divided on both sides, the new equation is also true: 44 ÷ 11 ÷ 2 = 4 ÷ 2

A. 49 − 7 = 42

49 − 7 ÷ 7 = 42 ÷ _____

B. 8 + 12 = 20

20 ÷ 4 = 8 + 12 ÷ _____

C. 100 ÷ 5 = 20

100 ÷ 5 ÷ 1 = _____

Name: _____ Date: _____

Pre-Algebra

#051. Identifying Operations to Balance Equations 1

For each equation, write *add, subtract, multiply, or divide* to show which **operation** you should do to balance the equation.

A. $17 + r = 9$ _____

B. $t + 71 = 4$ _____

C. $g - 42 = 36$ _____

D. $w - 18 = 437$ _____

#052. Identifying Operations to Balance Equations 2

For each equation, write *add, subtract, multiply, or divide* to show which **operation** you should do to balance the equation.

A. $s \div 42 = 462$ _____

B. $27 \times u = 108$ _____

C. $83 = 925 - v$ _____

D. $e \div 9 = 42$ _____

#053. Identifying Operations to Balance Equations 3

For each equation, write *add, subtract, multiply, or divide* to show which **operation** you should do to balance the equation.

A. $\frac{1}{2} \times u = \frac{3}{4}$ _____

B. $z \div 0.337 = 3.033$ _____

C. $d - \frac{7}{16} = \frac{1}{4}$ _____

D. $n + 4{,}326 = 5{,}325$ _____

#054. Isolating Variables to Balance Equations

When balancing equations, the best number to add, subtract, multiply, or divide both sides of the equation by is the number that will **isolate** the **variable** on one side of the equation.

Example: To isolate the variable in this equation: $p - 70 = 94$, the best number to add to both sides of the equation would be 70. Then $p - 70 + 70 = 94 + 70$. Simplify the equation: $p = 164$

A. To solve this equation, $b + 702 = 941$, what is the best number to subtract from both sides of the equation? _____

B. To solve this equation: $c \div \frac{1}{2} = \frac{7}{8}$, what is the best number to multiply both sides of the equation by? _____

Name: _____ Date: _____

Pre-Algebra

#055. Isolating Variables With Addition and Subtraction 1

To find the value of a **variable**, isolate it on one side of an equation by adding, subtracting, multiplying, or dividing both sides of the equation by the same amount.

Example:
$$n + 7 = 9$$
$$n + 7 - 7 = 9 - 7$$
$$n = 2$$

Isolate the variables by subtracting the same amount from both sides of the equation. Show your work.

A. $b + 48 = 52$ $b =$ _____

B. $c + 17 = 91$ $c =$ _____

C. $d + 21 = 49$ $d =$ _____

#056. Isolating Variables With Addition and Subtraction 2

Isolate the **variables** by adding the same amount to both sides of the equation. Show your work.

A. $e - 7 = 16$ $e =$ _____

B. $f - 9 = 83$ $f =$ _____

C. $g - 12 = 6$ $g =$ _____

#057. Isolating Variables With Multiplication and Division 1

Isolate the **variables** by dividing both sides of the equation by the same amount. Show your work.

A. $3 \times h = 9$ $h =$ _____

B. $4 \times j = 16$ $j =$ _____

C. $k \times 3 = 15$ $k =$ _____

#058. Isolating Variables With Multiplication and Division 2

Isolate the **variables** by multiplying both sides of the equation by the same amount. Show your work.

A. $m \div 4 = 3$ $m =$ _____

B. $n \div 3 = 7$ $n =$ _____

C. $p \div 8 = 5$ $p =$ _____

Name: _____ Date: _____

Pre-Algebra

#059. Isolating Variables Mixed Practice 1

Isolate the **variables**. Show your work.

A. $3 + 4 + r = 10$ $\qquad$ $r =$ _____

B. $17 - s = 4 + 12$ $\qquad$ $s =$ _____

C. $12 \times t = 6 \times 6$ $\qquad$ $t =$ _____

#060. Isolating Variables Mixed Practice 2

Find the value of the **variable** in each equation.

A. $76 - s = 48$ $\qquad$ $s =$ _____

B. $t - 438 = 291$ $\qquad$ $t =$ _____

C. $3^3 - b = 25$ $\qquad$ $b =$ _____

D. $r - 6^2 = 47$ $\qquad$ $r =$ _____

#061. Isolating Variables With Order of Operations

Find the value of the **variable** in each equation.

A. $(17 - h) \div 13 = 1$ $\qquad$ $h =$ _____

B. $e \div 36 = 8$ $\qquad$ $e =$ _____

C. $a \div (13 + 2) = 3$ $\qquad$ $a =$ _____

D. $7 = t \div 9$ $\qquad$ $t =$ _____

#062. Isolating Variables With Exponents

Find the value of the **variable** in each equation.

A. $16 = r^2$ $\qquad$ $r =$ _____

B. $e \times e = 5^2$ $\qquad$ $e =$ _____

C. $a = 6^3 + 1$ $\qquad$ $a =$ _____

D. $27 = d \times d \times d$ $\qquad$ $d =$ _____

Name: _____ Date: _____

Pre-Algebra

#063. Isolating Variables in Math Stories

Find the value of the **variable** in each equation.

A. Megan had an unknown number of photos. She divided them into 10 groups with 12 photos in each group. Let p equal the number of photos. Write and solve an equation to show how many photos she had. _____

B. LeRoy cut a length of string into 30 pieces, all the same length. If each piece of string was 13 inches long, how long was the string before he cut it? _____

C. If LeRoy cut that same string into 10 equal pieces instead, how long would each piece be? _____

#064. Step-by-Step

The park manager needs $5,387 to pay the balance on some new playground equipment. He has only $1,582 left in the budget. How much more does he need?

Write an equation for the math story. Use n for the unknown number:

_____

Isolate the variable. Rewrite the equation:

_____

Solve: n = _____

#065. Variables in Measurement

Write an algebraic expression  to show each **measurement**.

Example: The number of **inches** in an unknown number of **feet**. Let f = the variable.
Algebraic expression: $12 \times f$ (or $12f$)

A. The number of feet in an unknown number of **yards**. Let b = the variable.

Algebraic expression:

_____

B. The number of **ounces** in an unknown number of **pounds**. Let z = the variable.

Algebraic expression:

_____

#066. Variables in Distance Measurement

Write an algebraic expression to show each **measurement**.

A. The number of **feet** in an unknown number of **miles**: let c = the variable.

Algebraic expression:

_____

B. The number of **yards** in an unknown number of **inches**: let d = the variable.

Algebraic expression:

_____

Name: _____ Date: _____

Pre-Algebra

#067. Variables in Liquid Measurement

Write an algebraic expression to show each **measurement**.

A. The number of **cups** in an unknown number of **pints**:

Let e = the variable.

Algebraic expression:

_____

B. The number of **gallons** in an unknown number of **quarts**:

Let f = the variable.

Algebraic expression:

_____

#068. Variables in Time Measurement 1

Write an algebraic expression to show each **measurement**.

A. The number of **seconds** in an unknown number of **minutes**:

Let g = the variable.

Algebraic expression:

_____

B. The number of minutes in an unknown number of **days**:

Let h = the variable.

Algebraic expression:

_____

#069. Variables in Time Measurement 2

Write an algebraic expression to show each **measurement**.

A. The number of **days** in an unknown number of **weeks**:

Let j = the variable.

Algebraic expression:

_____

B. The number of weeks in an unknown number of days:

Let k = the variable.

Algebraic expression:

_____

#070. Variables in Formulas: Area of Rectangles

Area of a rectangle = length times width. This can be written as $A = lw$. l and w are variables.

Write the equation. Then find the area of each rectangle.

A. length = 5 feet, width = 7 feet

Equation: _____

Area = _____

7 ft.

5 ft.

B. length = 9 mm, width = 11 mm

Equation: _____

Area = _____

9 mm

11 mm

Name: _____ Date: _____

Pre-Algebra

#071. Variables in Formulas: Area of Triangles

Area of a triangle = $\frac{1}{2}$ base times height. This can be written as $A = \frac{1}{2}bh$. b and h are variables.

Write the equation. Then find the area of each triangle.

A. base = 6 feet, height = 7 feet
Equation: _____
Area = _____

B. base = 10 inches, height = 9 inches
Equation: _____
Area = _____

7 ft.
6 ft.

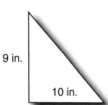
9 in.
10 in.

#072. Variables in Formulas: Volume of Rectangular Prisms

Volume of a rectangular prism = length times width times height. This can be written as $V = lwh$. l, w, and h are variables. Write the equation. Then find the volume of each rectangular prism.

A. 9-inch cube
Equation: _____
Volume = _____

B. l = 4 feet, w = 7 feet, h = 8 feet
Equation: _____
Volume = _____

C. l = 4 mm, w = 8 mm, h = 7 mm
Equation: _____
Volume = _____

#073. Variables in Formulas: Fill in the Blanks

Fill in the blanks with the correct word.

A. $A = lw$ means the _____ of a rectangle equals its _____ times its _____.

B. $A = \frac{1}{2}bh$ means _____
_____
_____.

C. $V = lwh$ means _____
_____
_____.

#074. Variables in Formulas: Word Problems

A. A garden measures 25 feet by 28 feet. What is its **area**?

_____

B. What is the area of a 4-inch square?

_____

C. What is the volume of a 7-inch cube?

_____

Name: _____ Date: _____

Pre-Algebra

#075. Multi-Step Operations With Variables 1

The 30 students in an advanced science class were ages 11, 12, and 13. One-half of the members were 12. Twenty percent were 11. The rest were 13. How many students of each age were in the class?

_____ 11-year-olds

_____ 12-year-olds

_____ 13-year-olds

#076. Multi-Step Operations With Variables 2

Ricardo worked at a pet store. They had 300 fish in several huge aquariums. Fifteen percent were clownfish. He counted 15 angelfish. The tanks included twice as many neon tetras as zebra fish. How many of each type were in the aquariums?

_____ clownfish

_____ angelfish

_____ neon tetras

_____ zebra fish

#077. Multi-Step Operations With Variables 3

At a tree farm, workers planted spruce, pine, and cedar saplings. They planted half as many spruce as pine. They planted three cedar for every four pine. They planted 96 spruce trees.

A.   How many trees did they plant in all?

_____

B.   How many cedar trees did they plant?

_____

#078. Multi-Step Operations With Variables 4

A.   Violet had a dozen and a half roses, 26 carnations, and 3 dozen daisies. She put 2 roses, 4 carnations, and 3 daisies in each bouquet. What was the maximum number of bouquets she could make using that combination of flowers?

_____

B.   If she wanted to use up the rest of the flowers and put a dozen flowers in each bouquet in any combination, how many more full bouquets could she make?

_____

Name: _____   Date: _____

Pre-Algebra

#079. Value of Variables Using Clues 1

What is the highest possible value of *b* if …

   b is less than 150, and

   b is divisible by 4, and

   all digits are even?

The highest possible

value of *b* = _____.

#080. Value of Variables Using Clues 2

What is the only possible value of *w* if …

   w is a number between 46 and 56, and

   w is an odd number, and

   w is evenly divisible by 3?

The only possible value of *w* = _____.

#081. Value of Variables Using Clues 3

What are two possible values of *n,* if …

   n is a multiple of 5, and

   n is divisible by 3, and

   the number in the ones place is 5, and

   n is less than 100?

Two possible values of *n* = _____ and _____.

#082. Value of Variables Using Clues 4

What is the value of *c*, if…

   c is greater than 3(4 + 12), and

   c is less than 50, and

   c is divisible by 7, and

   c is an odd number?

The only possible value of *c* = _____.

Name: _____ Date: _____

Pre-Algebra

#083. Equations With Two Variables 1

Example: Find the value of *y*.
Let *m* = 4.
$m + y = 13$
$y = 9$

Find the value of *y*. Let *m* = 8.

A. $m + y = 43$ *y* = _____

B. $y - m = 43$ *y* = _____

C. $m \times y = 56$ *y* = _____

D. $m \div y = 2$ *y* = _____

#084. Equations With Two Variables 2

Example: Find the value of *y*.
Let *m* = 4.
$m + y = 13$
$y = 9$

Find the value of *g*. Let $h = \frac{1}{2}$

A. $h + g = 7\frac{3}{4}$ *g* = _____

B. $g \div h = 14$ *g* = _____

C. $h \times g = 1$ *g* = _____

D. $g - h = 16\frac{3}{4}$ *g* = _____

#085. Solving Equations With Two Variables

Solve the equations. Let *c* = 4. Let *d* = 8.

A. $c + d =$ _____

B. $d \div c =$ _____

C. $c \times d =$ _____

D. $d \times 4 + c \div 4 =$ _____

#086. Writing Algebraic Expressions With Two Variables

Write an **algebraic expression** for each math story. Use *r* and *t* for **variables**.

A.   Todd had some science books. Rachel had some history books. Together, they had 73 books.

_____

B.   After Oscar lost some weight, he weighed 128 pounds.

_____

Name: _____ Date: _____

Pre-Algebra

#087. Factors

If a number divides evenly into another number, then it is a **factor** of that number.

Example: The numbers 1, 2, 3, 4, 6, and 12 all go into 12 evenly, so they are factors of 12.

Answer "yes" or "no" to the following.

A. Is 6 a factor of 30? _____

B. Is 4 a factor of 25? _____

C. Is 5 a factor of 28? _____

D. Is 11 a factor of 11? _____

Circle the numbers that are factors of the first number.

E. 8: 2   4   5   6   9

F. 17: 1   2   3   5   17

G. 32: 2   4   7   8   12

H. 25: 2   5   6   8   25

#088. Divisibility

Tests for **Divisibility:**
A number is divisible by 2 if the last digit is an even number.
A number is divisible by 3 if the digits add up to any multiple of 3 (e.g., 3, 6, 9,…).
A number is divisible by 5 if the last digit is 0 or 5.
A number is divisible by 10 if the last digit is 0.

Circle the numbers in each row that are…

A. divisible by 2:   5   8   10   30
    45   29   36   52   75   484

B. divisible by 3:   9   11   16   27
    33   50   24   18   423   780

C. divisible by 5:   11   35   70   28
    90   85   43   110   52   895

D. divisible by 10:   59   80   60   44
    20   12   70   118   220   350

#089. Prime and Composite Numbers

A number is **prime** if it is a whole number greater than 1 that has only 1 and itself as factors. A number is **composite** if it is a whole number greater than 1 that has at least one other factor besides 1 and itself.

In this grid, circle all the prime numbers and underline all the composite numbers.

1	2	3	4	5	6	7
8	9	10	11	12	13	14
15	16	17	18	19	20	21
22	23	24	25	26	27	28
29	30	31	32	33	34	35
36	37	38	39	40	41	42
43	44	45	46	47	48	49

#090. Prime Factorization

Every **composite number** can be factored into a product of **prime numbers**. To give the **prime factorization** of a composite number, first list the number as the product of any two numbers. Then, if either or both of those numbers is not prime, factor them. Continue until there are no more **factors** that are not prime.

Example: Find the prime factorization of 12:
$$12 = \underline{2} \times 6$$

Factor 6: $\underline{2} \times \underline{3}$
Therefore, the prime factorization of 12 is 2 × 2 × 3.

On your own paper, find the prime factorization for each number.

A. 44   **B.** 32   **C.** 45

D. 18   **E.** 50   **F.** 28

Name: _____   Date: _____

Pre-Algebra

#091. Find the Greatest Common Factor

The **Greatest Common Factor (GCF)** of two numbers is the largest number that is a **factor** of both numbers. One way to find the Greatest Common Factor of two numbers is to list all the factors of each number and then find the factors they have in common and see which is the largest.

Example: Find the GCF of 12 and 18
                6 is the largest, so it is the GCF.

| Factors of 12: 1, 2, 3, 4, 6, 12 |
| Factors of 18: 1, 2, 3, 6, 9, 18 |
| Factors in common: 1, 2, 3, 6 |

Use the method described to find the greatest common factor of these pairs.

A. 20 and 36   Factors of 20: _____   Factors of 36: _____

   Common factors: _____   GCF: ___

B. 21 and 28   Factors of 21: _____   Factors of 28: _____

   Common factors: _____   GCF: ___

C. 16 and 42   Factors of 16: _____   Factors of 42: _____

   Common factors: _____   GCF: ___

D. 24 and 48   Factors of 24: _____   Factors of 48: _____

   Common factors: _____   GCF: ___

#092. Least Common Multiple

Find the **Least Common Multiple (LCM)** by listing the **multiples** of both numbers until you find the first one they have in common (the lowest multiple).

Example: 3 and 5
   Multiples of 3: 3, 6, 9, 12, _15_, 18, 21
   Multiples of 5: 5, 10, _15_, 20, 25
   LCM: 15

Find the LCM of these pairs of numbers:

A. 4 and 6
   Multiples of 4: _____
   Multiples of 6: _____
   LCM: _____

B. 2 and 7
   Multiples of 2: _____
   Multiples of 7: _____
   LCM: _____

#093. Equivalent Fractions

Complete to get an **equivalent fraction**.

A. $\dfrac{4}{3} = \dfrac{\Box}{6}$ **B.** $\dfrac{1}{3} = \dfrac{\Box}{18}$

C. $\dfrac{3}{4} = \dfrac{\Box}{16}$ **D.** $\dfrac{3}{8} = \dfrac{\Box}{24}$

E. $\dfrac{5}{4} = \dfrac{\Box}{12}$ **F.** $\dfrac{4}{5} = \dfrac{\Box}{50}$

G. $\dfrac{5}{8} = \dfrac{\Box}{16}$ **H.** $\dfrac{7}{9} = \dfrac{\Box}{45}$

I. $\dfrac{1}{8} = \dfrac{\Box}{48}$ **J.** $\dfrac{1}{2} = \dfrac{4}{\Box}$

Name: _____ Date: _____

Pre-Algebra

#094. Writing Fractions in Lowest Terms

To write a **fraction** in **lowest terms**, divide both the numerator and the denominator by their **Greatest Common Factor**.

Example: $\dfrac{18}{24} = \dfrac{18 \div 6}{24 \div 6} = \dfrac{3}{4}$

Write each fraction in lowest terms.

A. $\dfrac{9}{18}$ = _____   B. $\dfrac{36}{42}$ = _____

C. $\dfrac{6}{30}$ = _____   D. $\dfrac{7}{56}$ = _____

E. $\dfrac{20}{60}$ = _____   F. $\dfrac{5}{45}$ = _____

#095. Adding Fractions With Like Denominators

To add fractions with **like denominators**, add the numerators, write the sum over the denominator, and then **reduce** the fraction to lowest terms if necessary.

Example: $\dfrac{5}{6} + \dfrac{3}{6} = \dfrac{5+3}{6} = \dfrac{8}{6} = 1\dfrac{2}{6} = 1\dfrac{1}{3}$

Add and put in simplest form.

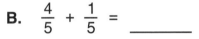

A. $\dfrac{2}{8} + \dfrac{3}{8}$ = _____

B. $\dfrac{4}{5} + \dfrac{1}{5}$ = _____

C. $\dfrac{2}{9} + \dfrac{4}{9}$ = _____

D. $\dfrac{6}{12} + \dfrac{7}{12}$ = _____

#096. Adding Fractions With Unlike Denominators

To add fractions with **unlike denominators**, find the **Least Common Multiple**, change to **equivalent fractions**, and then add.

Example: $\dfrac{3}{12} + \dfrac{4}{6}$ = ? 12 and 6 have 12 as the LCM. $\dfrac{3}{12}$ stays the same.

Change $\dfrac{4}{6}$ to $\dfrac{8}{12}$ Add: $\dfrac{3}{12} + \dfrac{8}{12} = \dfrac{11}{12}$

Add and put in simplest form.

A. $\dfrac{1}{2} + \dfrac{1}{3}$ = _____   B. $\dfrac{3}{8} + \dfrac{1}{4}$ = _____   C. $\dfrac{2}{5} + \dfrac{1}{3}$ = _____

D. $\dfrac{4}{5} + \dfrac{3}{8}$ = _____   E. $\dfrac{2}{5} + \dfrac{2}{6}$ = _____   F. $\dfrac{1}{8} + \dfrac{1}{16}$ = _____

G. $\dfrac{5}{9} + \dfrac{2}{6}$ = _____   H. $\dfrac{3}{12} + \dfrac{2}{4}$ = _____   I. $\dfrac{3}{4} + \dfrac{5}{7}$ = _____

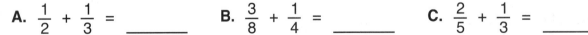
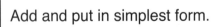

Name: _____   Date: _____

Pre-Algebra

#097. Subtracting Fractions With Like Denominators

To subtract fractions with **like denominators**, subtract the numerators, put the difference over the denominator, and **reduce** to lowest terms if necessary.

Example: $\dfrac{9}{15} - \dfrac{4}{15} = \dfrac{5}{15} = \dfrac{1}{3}$

Subtract and put in simplest form.

A. $\dfrac{5}{8} - \dfrac{1}{8} =$ _____

B. $\dfrac{4}{3} - \dfrac{2}{3} =$ _____

C. $\dfrac{12}{20} - \dfrac{4}{20} =$ _____

D. $\dfrac{11}{32} - \dfrac{3}{32} =$ _____

#098. Subtracting Fractions With Unlike Denominators

To subtract fractions with **unlike denominators**, find the **Least Common Multiple** of both denominators, change to **equivalent fractions** with that denominator, and subtract.

Example: $\dfrac{8}{12} - \dfrac{1}{3} = \dfrac{8}{12} - \dfrac{4}{12} = \dfrac{4}{12} = \dfrac{1}{3}$

Subtract and put in simplest form.

A. $\dfrac{12}{15} - \dfrac{2}{5} =$ _____

B. $\dfrac{7}{8} - \dfrac{3}{24} =$ _____

C. $\dfrac{3}{4} - \dfrac{1}{3} =$ _____

D. $\dfrac{7}{10} - \dfrac{1}{5} =$ _____

#099. Adding and Subtracting Fractions in Word Problems

Solve.

A. Mara's cookie recipe calls for $\frac{2}{3}$ cup of raisins and $\frac{1}{4}$ cup of nuts. Her nuts and raisins are mixed. How many cups should she put in her recipe?

_____

B. Philip brought out $\frac{9}{15}$ of his baseball cards. He gave away $\frac{1}{3}$ of these cards. What fraction of all his cards does he have left?

_____

#100. Multiplying Fractions

To multiply fractions, multiply the numerators to get the **numerator** of the product, multiply the denominators to get the **denominator** of the product, and **reduce** to lowest terms if necessary.

Example: $\dfrac{2}{3} \times \dfrac{1}{4} = \dfrac{2}{12} = \dfrac{1}{6}$

Multiply and put in simplest form.

A. $\dfrac{3}{2} \times \dfrac{1}{4} =$ _____

B $\dfrac{5}{8} \times \dfrac{4}{5} =$ _____

C. $\dfrac{5}{2} \times \dfrac{2}{5} =$ _____

D. $\dfrac{5}{12} \times \dfrac{3}{2} =$ _____

Name: _____   Date: _____

Pre-Algebra

#101. Dividing Fractions

To divide fractions, multiply the first fraction by the **reciprocal** of the second fraction. (Reminder: to find the reciprocal of a fraction, flip it upside down.)

Example: $\dfrac{3}{5} \div \dfrac{9}{10} = \dfrac{3}{5} \times \dfrac{10}{9} = \dfrac{30}{45} = \dfrac{2}{3}$

Divide and put in simplest form.

A. $\dfrac{5}{9} \div \dfrac{1}{3} =$ _____

B. $\dfrac{7}{5} \div \dfrac{7}{5} =$ _____

C. $\dfrac{3}{8} \div \dfrac{2}{3} =$ _____

D. $\dfrac{2}{7} \div \dfrac{4}{5} =$ _____

#102. Finding a Fraction of a Whole Number

To find a fraction of a number, multiply the number by the fraction and simplify.

Example: What is $\dfrac{2}{3}$ of 24?

Multiply $\dfrac{2}{3} \times 24 = \dfrac{2}{3} \times \dfrac{24}{1} = \dfrac{48}{3} = 16$

Solve.

A. $\dfrac{1}{4}$ of 16 = _____   B. $\dfrac{1}{3}$ of 27 = _____

C. $\dfrac{1}{5}$ of 45 = _____   D. $\dfrac{5}{6}$ of 30 = _____

E. $\dfrac{3}{4}$ of 36 = _____   F. $\dfrac{2}{5}$ of 10 = _____

G. $\dfrac{1}{2}$ of 38 = _____   H. $\dfrac{2}{3}$ of 18 = _____

#103. Canceling in Fractions

When multiplying fractions, you may **cancel** out numbers that are the same or that have common factors before multiplying.

Examples: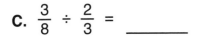

Show the cancellations and new factors. Then multiply.

A. $\dfrac{5}{16} \times \dfrac{4}{5} =$ _____   B. $\dfrac{8}{10} \times \dfrac{5}{4} =$ _____

C. $\dfrac{6}{5} \times \dfrac{15}{2} =$ _____   D. $\dfrac{5}{3} \times \dfrac{3}{5} =$ _____

#104. Review Adding and Subtracting Fractions/Test Taking

Fill in the bubble by the correct answer for each problem.

A. $\dfrac{2}{7} + \dfrac{3}{7}$ (a.) $\dfrac{5}{14}$ (b.) $\dfrac{5}{7}$

B. $\dfrac{2}{3} + \dfrac{3}{4}$ (a.) $1\dfrac{5}{12}$ (b.) $\dfrac{5}{7}$

C. $\dfrac{3}{5} + \dfrac{2}{4}$ (a.) $1\dfrac{1}{10}$ (b.) $\dfrac{5}{20}$

D. $\dfrac{7}{9} - \dfrac{4}{9}$ (a.) $\dfrac{11}{9}$ (b.) $\dfrac{1}{3}$

E. $\dfrac{4}{5} - \dfrac{1}{4}$ (a.) $\dfrac{3}{20}$ (b.) $\dfrac{11}{20}$

Name: _____ Date: _____

Pre-Algebra

#105. Review Multiplying and Dividing Fractions/Test Taking

Fill in the bubble by the correct answer for each problem.

A. $\frac{2}{3} \times \frac{3}{4}$ (a.) $\frac{1}{2}$ (b.) $\frac{5}{12}$

B. $\frac{4}{5} \times \frac{1}{5}$ (a.) $\frac{5}{25}$ (b.) $\frac{4}{25}$

C. $\frac{7}{8} \div \frac{5}{16}$ (a.) $2\frac{4}{5}$ (b.) $1\frac{7}{8}$

D. $\frac{3}{5} \div \frac{2}{5}$ (a.) $\frac{6}{25}$ (b.) $1\frac{1}{2}$

E. $\frac{0}{4} \div \frac{5}{6}$ (a.) 0 (b.) $\frac{5}{24}$

#106. Multiplying and Dividing by 10; 100; 1,000; etc.

To multiply by a **power of 10**, move the decimal to the right as many places as there are 0's in the power of 10.

To divide by a power of 10, move the decimal to the left as many places as there are 0's in the power of 10.

Multiply or divide.

A. 134.6799×100 B. 33.00085×10

_____   _____

C. $0.45 \times 10,000$ D. 28.1919×100

_____   _____

E. $27.007 \div 100$ F. $21,345.99 \div 1,000$

_____   _____

#107. Scientific Notation

To write numbers in **scientific notation**, move the decimal so that you get a number greater than 1 but less than 10. Then count the number of places you moved the decimal (to the right or left). Multiply the number between 1 and 10 by 10 with an **exponent** indicating how many places you moved the decimal. Use a **positive exponent** if you moved the decimal to the left and a **negative exponent** if you moved it to the right.

Examples: $42,000,000 = 4.2 \cdot 10^7$ $0.0000975 = 9.75 \cdot 10^{-5}$

Give the missing exponent.

A. $23,700 = 2.37 \cdot 10^?$ _____   B. $0.00339 = 3.39 \cdot 10^?$ _____

Write each number in scientific notation. Use a dot to represent multiplication.

C. $456,000,000$ _____   D. 0.000000946 _____

E. The sun is 93,000,000 miles from Earth. _____

F. The water level of the ocean rises about 0.0029 of a foot every day. _____

Name: _____ Date: _____

Pre-Algebra

#108. Adding and Subtracting Decimals

To add or subtract, line up the numbers at the **decimal points**, and then add or subtract as normal.

Examples:

$$\begin{array}{r} 1 \\ 49.2 \\ + \ 3.51 \\ \hline 52.71 \end{array}$$

$$\begin{array}{r} 2 \ 10 \\ \cancel{3}.094 \\ - \ 0.72 \\ \hline 2.374 \end{array}$$

Add or subtract. Write the answers on the lines.

A. 7.3 + 2.9

_____

B. 13.0 + 9.41

_____

C. 8.3 + 6.9 + 8.5

_____

D. 3.376 + 28.6

_____

E. 2.93 – 0.48

_____

F. 5.74 – 3.8

_____

G. 372.778 – 39.81

_____

H. 2.078 – 0.1

_____

#109. Multiplying Decimals

To multiply decimals, multiply the same as for whole numbers. Then count how many total **decimal places** are in both numbers and place the **decimal point** in the **product** with that many places after the decimal point.

Example: 3.16 × 1.153 (5 decimal places)

316 × 1153 = 364348

Answer: 3.64348

Multiply.

A. 25.3 × 8.16 = _____

B. 569.1 × 4.2 = _____

C. 7.2 × 0.58 = _____

D. 35.02 × 16 = _____

E. 18.3 × 61.4 = _____

F. 12.8 × 0.155 = _____

#110. Dividing Decimals by Whole Numbers

To divide decimals by whole numbers, divide the same as with whole numbers, but place the **decimal point** directly above the decimal point in the **dividend**.

Example: $2\overline{)4.66}$ with quotient 2.33

Divide.

A. $3\overline{)3.75}$

B. $5\overline{)85.60}$

C. $4\overline{)562.464}$

D. $2\overline{)0.6894}$

#111. Dividing Decimals by Decimals

To divide a decimal by another decimal, first move the **decimal point** in the **divisor** to the right until you get a whole number. Then move the decimal point in the **dividend** the same number of places you moved the decimal point in the divisor. Then divide the same as dividing decimals by whole numbers.

Example: $3.2\overline{)6.464} \longrightarrow 32\overline{)64.64}$ with quotient 2.02

Divide. Work the problems on your own paper.

A. $0.11\overline{)16.83}$

B. $0.08\overline{)1.48}$

C. $1.2\overline{)3.906}$

D. $2.8\overline{)23.24}$

Name: _____   Date: _____

Pre-Algebra

#112. Review Decimals/Test Taking

Fill in the bubble by the correct answer for each problem. Select the correct answer showing the decimal rounded to the nearest hundredth.

A. 54.6712   (a.) 54.68   (b.) 54.67

B. 358.13779   (a.) 358.14   (b.) 358.13

Select the correct answer showing each fraction changed to a decimal.

C. $\frac{2}{10}$ (a.) 0.102   (b.) 0.20

D. $\frac{2}{4}$ (a.) 0.5   (b.) 0.25

E. $\frac{3}{4}$ (a.) 0.75   (b.) 0.34

F. $\frac{6}{8}$ (a.) 0.65   (b.) 0.75

#113. Review +, −, x, ÷ Decimals

Solve.

A. 33.674 + 282.9 = _____

B. 987.3 − 22.65 = _____

C. (56.4)(32.11) = _____

D. 1.98 × 31.3 = _____

E. $7\overline{)28.7}$ **F.** $0.05\overline{)3.650}$

#114. Integers and Absolute Value

Integers are the set of whole numbers and their opposites (positive and negative numbers).

Write "Yes" or "No" to indicate if each of these is an integer.

A. -18 _____   **B.** 969 _____

C. $\frac{1}{2}$ _____   **D.** 687.5 _____

Write the opposite of each number.

E. 14 ____   **F.** -3 ____   **G.** -27 ____

Find the absolute value.

H. $|42|$ _____   **I.** $|-578|$ _____

Write an integer to represent each situation.

J. going up 3 floors _____

K. Losing 12 yards _____

L. 7 degrees below zero _____

#115. Comparing Numbers

Use the number line to help you compare the numbers. Write <, >, or = to describe how the numbers are compared.

-30 -25 -20 -15 -10 -5 0 5 10 15 20 25 30

A. 6 ____ 9   **B.** -17 ____ -14

C. $|-22|$ ____ 0   **D.** -11 ____ -12

E. $|25|$ ____ $|-25|$ **F.** 28.5 ____ 30

G. -6 ____ $|-6|$ **H.** 4.5 ____ 4.6

I. $|-18|$ ____ $|19|$ **J.** 0 ____ $|-13|$

Name: _____ Date: _____

Pre-Algebra

#116. Adding Integers

Remember, to add **integers** that have the same sign, just add their **absolute values** and give the result the same sign as the integers. To add integers that have different signs, subtract their absolute values and give the result the sign of the larger integer.

Find each sum.

A. 15 + (-12) = _____

B. (-24) + 18 = _____

C. 42 + (-8) = _____

D. 16 + 14 = _____

E. (-15) + 15 = _____

F. (-11) + (-19) = _____

G. $\left| -39 \right| + \left| 10 \right|$ = _____

Bonus: 22 + (-10) + (-16) + 5 = _____

#117. Subtracting Integers

Remember, to subtract an **integer**, just add its **opposite**.

Find each difference.

A. 11 – 8 = _____

B. 12 – (-4) = _____

C. (-8) – 4 = _____

D. 36 – 20 = _____

E. 9 – (-3) = _____

F. 38 – 48 = _____

G. 10 – (-16) = _____

H. (-2) – (-2) = _____

I. (-15) – 5 = _____

J. (-18) – (-40) = _____

Bonus: 25 – (-7) – (-4) = _____

#118. Multiplying Integers

Remember, when you multiply two **integers** with the same sign, the result will be **positive**. When you multiply two integers with different signs, the result will be **negative**.

Find each product.

A. 6 × 4 = _____

B. 11 × (-4) = _____

C. (-5) × (-8) = _____

D. (-7) × 6 = _____

E. (-8) × (-8) = _____

F. (-14) × 0 = _____

G. 15 × 10 = _____

H. (-3) × 7 = _____

I. 9 × (-8) = _____

Bonus: 5 × (-4) × (-3) = _____

#119. Dividing Integers

Remember, when you divide two **integers** with the same sign, the result is **positive**. When you divide two integers with different signs, the result is **negative**.

Find each quotient.

A. 18 ÷ 3 = _____

B. 28 ÷ (-4) = _____

C. (-33) ÷ 11 = _____

D. 16 ÷ 8 = _____

E. (-27) ÷ 9 = _____

F. (-32) ÷ (-8) = _____

G. (-20) ÷ (-5) = _____

H. 45 ÷ 15 = _____

I. $\dfrac{-96}{8}$ = _____   **J.** $\dfrac{(-42)}{(-7)}$ = _____

Bonus: 132 ÷ (-11) ÷ 4 = _____

Name: _____   Date: _____

Pre-Algebra

#120. Order of Operations

Remember, when an expression has several components, use this **order of operations**:
1. Perform operations inside parentheses or brackets.
2. Multiply and divide from left to right.
3. Add and subtract from left to right.

Solve.

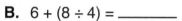

A. $(3 \times 4) - 9 =$ _____

B. $6 + (8 \div 4) =$ _____

C. $(-8) + (10 - 4) + 2 =$ _____

D. $6 \div 3 \times 5 =$ _____

E. $(3 + 5) + (6 + 7) =$ _____

F. $(-11) - (4 + 4) =$ _____

G. $(16 \div 4) \times (5 + 5) =$ _____

H. $22 - 7(3 + 3) =$ _____

Bonus: $(16 \times 2) + (8 \div 4) - (17 - 9) =$ _____

#121. Evaluating Variable Expressions

To evaluate a **variable expression** for given terms, substitute the numbers for the variables.

Example: $3n$ Evaluate the expression for n = C. Substitute 3 for n. $3(3) = 9$

Evaluate each expression for $n = 5$, $x = 3$, and $y = 2$.

A. $n + 5 =$ _____   **B.** $x - (-4) =$ _____

C. $3y =$ _____   **D.** $3n - x =$ _____

E. $4x - 4 =$ _____   **F.** $3y - y =$ _____

G. $\dfrac{n + x}{y} =$ _____   **H.** $\dfrac{12 - y}{n} =$ _____

I. $x^2 =$ _____   **J.** $y^3 - 1 =$ _____

K. $(6n + x - y) =$ _____

L. $n - 5 + (x + 4) =$ _____

#122. Exponents

A repeated **factor** is called the **base**, and the **exponent** tells how many times the factor is multiplied by itself.

Example: 7^4 7 (base), ^{4} (exponent)
$$7^4 = 7 \cdot 7 \cdot 7 \cdot 7 = 2,401$$

Note: The dot or parentheses will be used to represent multiplication from this point on to avoid confusion with the variable x.

Write each expression using a single exponent.

A. $6 \cdot 6 \cdot 6 =$ _____   **B.** $-5 \cdot -5 =$ _____

C. $x \cdot x \cdot x \cdot x \cdot x =$ _____

D. $(-7)(-7)(-7) =$ _____

Write each expression as a product of repeated factors.

E. $11^2 =$ _____   **F.** $-4^4 =$ _____

#123. Multiplying and Dividing Exponents

To **multiply** numbers or variables with the same **base**, add the **exponents**. To **divide** numbers or variables with the same base, subtract the exponents.

Examples: $2^2 \cdot 2^4 = 2^{2+4} = 2^6$
$$5^9 \div 5^4 = 5^{9-4} = 5^5$$

Write each expression using a single exponent.

A. $7^3 \cdot 7^5 =$ _____   **B.** $9^8 \div 9^4 =$ _____

C. $r^6 \cdot r^3 =$ _____   **D.** $m^7 \div m^2 =$ _____

Use a calculator to evaluate.

E. $3^4 \cdot 3^3 =$ _____   **F.** $6^8 \div 6^3 =$ _____

G. $2^5 \cdot 2^4 =$ _____   **H.** $\dfrac{7^7}{7^4} =$ _____

Name: _____ Date: _____

Pre-Algebra

#124. Negative Exponents

A **negative exponent** is made positive by moving the exponent from the **numerator** to the **denominator**.

Examples: $6^{-4} = \dfrac{1}{6^4}$ $\qquad 2b^{-3} = \dfrac{2}{b^3}$

Write each expression using positive exponents.

A. 8^{-2} _____ **B.** n^{-15} _____

C. 5^{-5} _____ **D.** xy^{-3} _____

Write each fraction as an expression with negative exponents.

E. $\dfrac{1}{4^6}$ _____ **F.** $\dfrac{1}{11^2}$ _____

G. $\dfrac{x}{y^5}$ _____ **H.** $\dfrac{m}{n^4}$ _____

#125. Order of Operations

Remember the **order of operations**:
1. Perform anything in parentheses or brackets first.
2. Evaluate the exponents.
3. Multiply and divide from left to right.
4. Add and subtract from left to right.

Evaluate each expression.

A. $3^2 + (3 \cdot 4) - 6 =$ _____

B. $7 + 8 - 3^2 =$ _____

C. $[18 - 3] \cdot 3 - 5 =$ _____

D. $(2 + 8) \div 2 \cdot 4^2 =$ _____

Evaluate each expression for the given number.

E. $a^2 + (9 - 4); \ a = 2$ _____

F. $(x - 3)^3 + 16 - (5 + x) \cdot 2; \ x = 4$ _____

G. $3^m + (2 + 1)^{m-1}; \ m = 2$ _____

#126. Properties of Numbers

Match the examples with which property of numbers is represented.

_____ **A.** Commutative Property

_____ **B.** Associative Property

_____ **C.** Distributive Property

_____ **D.** Identity Property

a. $5 + 0 = 5 \qquad n + 0 = n$

b. $4 + 5 = 5 + 4 \qquad x + y = y + x$

c. $3(2 + 3) = (3 \cdot 2) + (3 \cdot 3)$

$a(b + c) = (a \cdot b) + (a \cdot c)$

d. $(2 + 3) + 6 = 2 + (3 + 6)$

$(x + y) + z = x + (y + z)$

#127. Commutative Property

The **commutative property** states that when you change the order of **addends** or **factors**, you do not change the result. Addition and multiplication have this property.

Examples: $4 + 7 = 7 + 4 \qquad 3 \cdot 8 = 8 \cdot 3$

$x + y = y + x \qquad x \cdot y = y \cdot x$

Write each equation in a different way by using the commutative property.

A. $c + 7 = 15$ _____

B. $3 \cdot d = 12$ _____

C. $8 + m = 10$ _____

D. $k \cdot 6 = 30$ _____

E. $x + 11 = 21$ _____

F. $r \cdot 4 = 16$ _____

G. $y + x + z = 28$ _____

Name: _____ Date: _____

Pre-Algebra

#128. Associative Property

The **associative property** states that changing the groupings of **addends** or **factors** does not change the result. Addition and multiplication have this property.

Examples:

$(3 + 8) + 4 = 3 + (8 + 4)$ $(4 \cdot 2) \cdot 6 = 4 \cdot (2 \cdot 6)$

$(x + y) + z = x + (y + z)$ $(a \cdot b) \cdot c = a \cdot (b \cdot c)$

Place parentheses in these expressions to make the computation easier. Then compute.

A. $45 + 55 + 38$ _____

B. $43 + 92 + 8$ _____

C. $31 + 9 + 15 + 5$ _____

D. $4 \cdot 5 \cdot 7$ _____

E. $48 \cdot 2 \cdot 5$ _____

F. $10 \cdot 10 \cdot 15 \cdot 10$ _____

G. $-2 \cdot 5 \cdot 96$ _____

#129. Distributive Property

The **distributive property** states that if x, y, and z are any numbers, then $x(y + z) = xy + xz$ and $x(y - z) = xy - xz$.

Examples: $4(3 + 2) = (4 \cdot 3) + (4 \cdot 2) = 20$
$3(7 - 3) = (3 \cdot 7) - (3 \cdot 3) = 12$

Rewrite each expression using the distributive property. Do not simplify.

A. $5(4 + 5)$ _____

B. $w(4 + 9)$ _____

C. $3(4b + 3c)$ _____

Simplify each expression by using the distributive property.

D. $2(v + 3) + 7v$ _____

E. $5g + 6(2g + 3)$ _____

F. $7s + 4s + 4(2s + 5)$ _____

#130. Properties of Zero and One

Properties of zero and one can make computations much simpler.

Identity property of addition: The sum of any number and 0 is that number. $n + 0 = n$

Identity property of multiplication: The product of any number and 1 is that number. $n \cdot 1 = n$

Multiplication property of 0: The product of any number and 0 is 0. $n \cdot 0 = 0$

Solve each expression mentally.

A. $47 + (16 - 16) =$ _____

B. $\frac{87}{87} \cdot 65 =$ _____

C. $(72 \cdot 0) \cdot 13 =$ _____

D. $(18 \cdot 0) + 46 =$ _____

E. $(368 - 368) \cdot 455 =$ _____

F. $32 \cdot [7 - (3 + 3)] =$ _____

#131. Combining Like Terms

Combine **like terms** to simplify.

A. $2x + 3y + 3x$ _____

B. $t + 4s - 2s$ _____

C. $3m - 6n + 2m + 4n$ _____

D. $2a - 4b + 3a$ _____

E. $7c - 4d + 3c$ _____

F. $2f - 4g + 6g - 3f$ _____

G. $j - h + 3j - 4h$ _____

H. $5w + 3w + 2w + 7v$ _____

I. $3y - y + 4z + 2z$ _____

J. $6a + 2b + 3c - 2c + 3b$ _____

K. $4h + 2i + 3j - 2h - i$ _____

L. $m + n + p - m + 2n$ _____

Name: _____   Date: _____

Pre-Algebra

#132. Simplifying Variable Expressions

Simplify each expression.

A. $4(x + 3)$ _____

B. $8(m - 6)$ _____

C. $3(2b - 1)$ _____

D. $-4n(2 + 2)$ _____

E. $2(x + 4) - x$ _____

F. $5c + 3(c - 2)$ _____

G. $6(2m - 4) - 2$ _____

H. $9(g + h)$ _____

I. $2(d + 4) + c - 1$ _____

J. $-5x - 4y + 2(3y - 1)$ _____

K. $-4 + 3(b - 2)$ _____

L. $5(a + b) - a - b$ _____

#133. Solving Equations by Subtracting

To solve an equation, you use **inverse operations** to isolate the variable on one side. Use subtraction (the inverse operation of addition) to isolate the variable in these equations.

A. $y + 9 = 12$ _____

B. $6 + m = 11$ _____

C. $10 + b = 15$ _____

D. $z + 3 = 7$ _____

E. $n + 6 = 20$ _____

F. $x + 4 = 4$ _____

G. $8 + m = 4$ _____

H. $z + 6 = -2$ _____

I. $w + 7 = 7$ _____

J. $n + 5 = -1$ _____

#134. Solving Equations by Adding

To solve an equation, you use **inverse operations** to isolate the variable on one side. Use addition (the inverse operation of subtraction) to isolate the variable in these equations.

A. $b - 4 = 2$ _____

B. $m - 6 = 5$ _____

C. $n - 11 = 0$ _____

D. $(-6) + y = 4$ _____

E. $a - 8 = 1$ _____

F. $(-4) + v = 0$ _____

G. $(-2) + t = 5$ _____

H. $c - 3 = 2$ _____

I. $m - 17 = 20$ _____

J. $b - \dfrac{1}{2} = \dfrac{1}{2}$ _____

#135. Problem Solving With Equations

Write an equation to represent the situation, and then solve by adding or subtracting.

A. Mike earned $28 on Monday. On Wednesday, he earned some more money. He earned $42 total. How much did Mike earn on Wednesday?

_____

B. Allysa made some cookies. She took 24 to school for a bake sale. She has 30 left. How many cookies did she make?

_____

C. Milo did 58 homework problems right after school. He did the rest in the evening. If he did 80 problems all together, how many did he do in the evening?

_____

Name: _____   Date: _____

Pre-Algebra

#136. Solving Equations by Dividing

To solve an equation, you use **inverse operations** to isolate the variable on one side. Use division (the inverse operation of multiplication) to isolate the variable in these equations.

A. $6m = 48$ _____

B. $4t = 16$ _____

C. $8a = 72$ _____

D. $5x = 55$ _____

E. $7p = 21$ _____

F. $9z = 90$ _____

G. $-4y = 28$ _____

H. $-7g = -42$ _____

I. $9t = 3$ _____

J. $100j = 25$ _____

#137. Solving Equations by Multiplying

Use multiplication (the inverse operation of division) to isolate the variable in these equations.

A. $\dfrac{x}{4} = 5$ _____

B. $\dfrac{m}{2} = 8$ _____

C. $\dfrac{g}{5} = 10$ _____

D. $\dfrac{n}{6} = 0$ _____

E. $\dfrac{w}{-3} = -4$ _____

F. $\dfrac{k}{-2} = 6$ _____

G. $\dfrac{h}{15} = 3$ _____

#138. Solving Equations by Dividing or Multiplying

Choose the appropriate **inverse operation** to solve these equations.

A. $\dfrac{a}{-3} = 5$ _____

B. $6b = 36$ _____

C. $8n = 48$ _____

D. $\dfrac{w}{7} = 5$ _____

E. $\dfrac{y}{4} = 9$ _____

F. $3x = 36$ _____

G. $\dfrac{d}{-4} = -4$ _____

#139. Problem Solving Using Equations

Write an equation to represent the situation, and then solve by dividing or multiplying.

A. Gregorio has to make 84 cookies for scout camp. How many dozen cookies is that?

_____

B. Zola bought 9 candy bars. She spent $4.05. How much did each bar cost?

_____

C. Jahim will buy a video game that costs $54 in 6 weeks. How much must he save each week to have enough money by then?

_____

D. Tina sold 8 pencils at $1.95 each. How much money did she earn?

_____

Name: _____ Date: _____

Pre-Algebra

#140. Solving Two-Step Equations 1

To solve equations, sometimes it is necessary to perform more than one step. Solve these equations using whatever **inverse operations** are needed.

A. $6x - 5 = 7$ _____

B. $-5 = 3y - 14$ _____

C. $4m + 4 = 16$ _____

D. $3d - 4 = 8$ _____

E. $-7 = 9 + 2h$ _____

F. $11n - 6 = 60$ _____

G. $32 = 12b - 4$ _____

H. $18 = 2f + 2$ _____

I. $5a + 9 = 29$ _____

J. $3p - 15 = -6$ _____

#141. Solving Two-Step Equations 2

Solve.

A. $\dfrac{t}{4} - 1 = 10$ _____

B. $\dfrac{b}{3} + 8 = 13$ _____

C. $6 - \dfrac{x}{2} = 2$ _____

D. $12 + \dfrac{m}{7} = 15$ _____

E. $-11 + \dfrac{z}{5} = -7$ _____

F. $\dfrac{w}{-3} + 8 = 5$ _____

G. $\dfrac{y}{9} - 4 = 6$ _____

#142. Problem Solving by Writing and Solving Equations

Write an **equation** for each problem and solve.

A. If you multiply a number by 8 and add 12, you get 60. What is the number?

_____

B. Three more than 7 times a number is 38. What is the number?

_____

C. The sum of 5 times a number and 10 is 55. What is the number?

_____

D. If you divide a number by 4 and add 7, you get 15. What is the number?

_____

#143. Problem Solving Using Equations/Test Practice

Fill in the bubble next to the correct equation that would allow you to solve the problem.

A. If you divide a number by 7 and take away 4, you get 4. Which equation would you use?

   (a.) $\dfrac{n}{7} - 4 = 4$ (b.) $\dfrac{4}{7} - n = 4$

B. Five more than 4 times a number is 33. Which equation would you use?

   (a.) $4n + 5 = 33$ (b.) $4n - 5 = 33$

C. Three less than a number divided by 6 is 3. Which equation would you use?

   (a.) $\dfrac{n}{6} - 3 = 3$ (b.) $\dfrac{6}{n} - 3 = 3$

Name: _____ Date: _____

Pre-Algebra

#144. Simplifying and Solving Equations 1

First simplify each equation by combining **like terms**, and then solve.

A. $x + 4x - 3 = 22$ _____

B. $2n + 3n - 7 = 13$ _____

C. $6b + 9 - 2b = 21$ _____

D. $t + 3t = -8$ _____

E. $3s + 10 - 5s = -2$ _____

F. $y - 7 - 6y = -47$ _____

G. $4t + 16 + 2t = 28$ _____

H. $46 - 2r + 3r = 53$ _____

I. $3m + 12 - m = 78$ _____

J. $-3p + 5p + 4 = -6$ _____

#145. Simplifying and Solving Equations 2

First simplify each equation, and then solve.

A. $2(n - 4) + 3n = 37$ _____

B. $4z + 3(z + 2) = 34$ _____

C. $-3(2t - 4) + 11 = -7$ _____

D. $7(k - 6) + 8 = -13$ _____

E. $2c + 2(c - 6) = 72$ _____

F. $9(h - 1) + h = 11$ _____

G. $8(g + 2) + 3(g - 2) = 76$

_____

H. $6(j - 7) + 5(2j + 3) = 37$

_____

#146. Inequalities

Circle the numbers below that are a solution of $x \le -2$.

A. -5   **B.** 3   **C.** 0

D. -2   **E.** -1

Write an **inequality** for each sentence.

F. Joe will need to earn at least $46 to buy his bike. _____

G. The maximum number of passengers that the plane will hold is 200. _____

H. To ride the roller coaster, you must be at least 52 inches tall. _____

I. Each bag must weigh at least 6 pounds. _____

J. There are fewer than a dozen cookies left in the jar. _____

#147. Graphing Inequalities 1

Write an **inequality** for each graph.

A. _____

B. _____

C. _____

D. _____

Name: _____ Date: _____

Pre-Algebra

#148. Graphing Inequalities 2

Graph each of these **inequalities**.

A. $y < 4$

B. $t \geq -1$

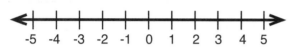

C. $a > -3$

D. $g \leq 5$

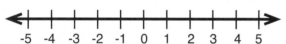

#149. Solving Inequalities by Adding and Subtracting

Solve each **inequality** by adding or subtracting. Then **graph** the solution.

A. $x + 2 < 4$ _____

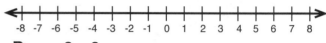

B. $y - 3 > 2$ _____

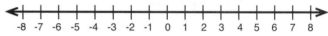

C. $7 + a \leq 3$ _____

D. $r - 6 < 0$ _____

E. $s + 5 \geq 3$ _____

#150. Solving Inequalities by Dividing or Multiplying

Solve each **inequality** by dividing or multiplying. Then **graph** the solution.

A. $6q \geq 24$ _____

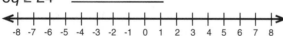

B. $5n < 15$ _____

C. $4c > -4$ _____

D. $\dfrac{x}{2} \leq 1$ _____

E. $\dfrac{s}{3} < 2$ _____

#151. Review Solving Inequalities/ Test Taking

Fill in the bubble next to the correct solution to each inequality.

A. $t - 7 < -4$ (a.) $t < -3$ (b.) $t < 3$

B. $x + 3 \geq 5$ (a.) $x \geq 2$ (b.) $x \leq 2$

C. $2b - 5 < 7$ (a.) $b < 6$ (b.) $b < 12$

D. $\dfrac{w}{4} \leq 1$ (a.) $w \leq \dfrac{1}{4}$ (b.) $w \leq 4$

E. $3(r + 1) > 0$ (a.) $r > 1$ (b.) $r > -1$

F. $\dfrac{m}{2} + 6 < 9$ (a.) $m < 6$ (b.) $m < \dfrac{3}{2}$

Name: _____ Date: _____

Pre-Algebra

#152. Graphing in the Coordinate Plane: Identifying Points

Name the point at each **coordinate**.

A. (-2, -6) _____   **B.** (4, 4) _____

C. (3, -2) _____   **D.** (0, 5) _____

E. (-3, 3) _____   **F.** (1, -3) _____

Give the coordinates for each point.

G. B _____   **H.** N _____

I. J _____   **J.** G _____

K. I _____   **L.** H _____

M. D _____   **N.** E _____

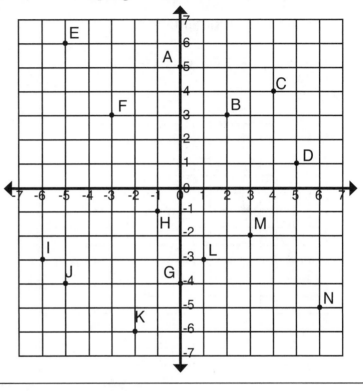

#153. Graphing in the Coordinate Plane: Draw a Figure

Draw this figure of a square inside a square inside a square by plotting the following points on the graph and then connecting the sides of each square.

Largest square:
    (-6, 6)   (6, 6)
    (-6, -6)   (6, -6)

Middle square:
    (-4, 4)   (4, 4)
    (-4, -4)   (4, -4)

Smallest square:
    (-2, 2)   (2, 2)
    (-2, -2)   (2, -2)

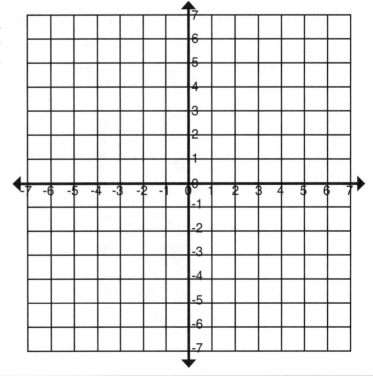

Name: _____ Date: _____

Pre-Algebra

#154. Graphing Linear Equations

Graph each **linear equation**.

A. $y = -2x + 1$ **B.** $y = 3x - 2$

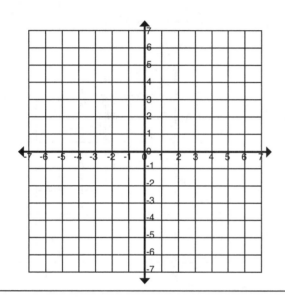

#155. Finding Slope From a Graph

To find the **slope** of a line, choose two points on the line and count the **rise** and the **run** between those two points. Write them as a **ratio** (fraction). Find the slope of each line.

A. _____   **B.** _____

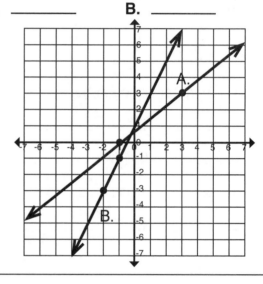

#156. Slope

Reminder: The **slope** of a line is how steep it is. It is calculated as the ratio of $\dfrac{rise}{run}$.

Start at the bottom left corner of the graph paper and make a staircase with the indicated **rise** and **run**. Then draw a line touching the tips of each stair.

A. rise = 1
run = 1
(slope of 1)

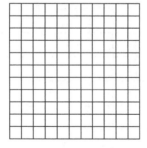

B. rise = 3
run = 2
(slope of $\dfrac{3}{2}$)

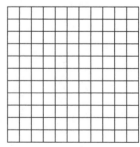

C. rise = 2
run = 1
(slope of $\dfrac{2}{1}$ = 2)

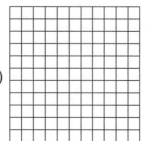

D. rise = 1
run = 2
(slope of $\dfrac{1}{2}$)

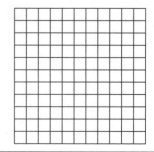

Name: _____   Date: _____

Pre-Algebra

#157. Negative Slope and Zero Slope

A line moving upward from left to right has a **positive slope**. A line moving downward from left to right has a **negative slope**. If a line is horizontal it has a **zero slope**. Find the slope of each line.

A. _____

B. _____

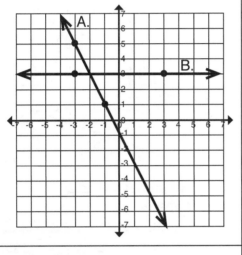

#158. Finding Slope Using Two Points

You can find the **slope** of a line by subtracting the *y*-coordinates and the *x*-coordinates and putting them in a ratio: $\frac{y_2 - y_1}{x_2 - x_1}$.

Using the coordinates given, find the slope of each line.

A. (0, 3) and (3, 2) _____

B. (-1, 3) and (0, 0) _____

C. (-2, -1) and (2, 1) _____

D. (-3, 0) and (3, 2) _____

E. (-2, -2) and (2, 2) _____

F. (0, 1) and (2, 3) _____

#159. Graphing Linear Equations Using Slope

You can **graph a line** if you know one point on that line and the **slope**. To do so, first **plot the point**. Then find other points on the line by moving up/down and over according to the **rise** and **run** indicated in the slope.

Graph the line that has the given point and slope.

A. (-1, -3), $\frac{2}{3}$

B. (0, 2), $-\frac{1}{2}$

C. (0, -4), $\frac{3}{2}$

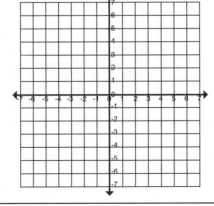

#160. Finding *x*- and *y*-Intercepts

To find the **x-intercept** for a line, let $y = 0$ and solve for *x*. To find the **y-intercept** of a line, let $x = 0$ and solve for *y*. You could then plot those two points and connect them to show the line.

Find the *x*- and *y*-intercepts to help you graph each line. Use your own graph paper.

A. $y = 2x + 2$
   x-intercept _____
   y-intercept _____

B. $y = -x + 1$
   x-intercept _____
   y-intercept _____

C. $y = 3x - 3$
   x-intercept _____
   y-intercept _____

Name: _____ Date: _____

Pre-Algebra

#161. Equations in Slope-Intercept Form

When an equation is in the form $y = mx + b$, then m indicates the **slope**, and b indicates the **y-intercept**.

Example: $y = \frac{3}{4}x + 7$ The slope is $\frac{3}{4}$ and the y-intercept is 7.

Tell what the slope and y-intercept of each equation is.

A. $y = \frac{1}{3}x - 6$ slope _____
                          y-intercept _____

B. $y = -3x + 4$ slope _____
                          y-intercept _____

C. $y = -\frac{2}{5}x - \frac{1}{2}$ slope _____
                          y-intercept _____

D. $y = 4x - 2$ slope _____
                          y-intercept _____

#162. Writing an Equation for a Line

Use the **slope-intercept form** ($y = mx + b$) to help write an equation for a line. First, find the **y-intercept** of the line, and then find the **slope**. Use that information to write an equation with the form $y = mx + b$.

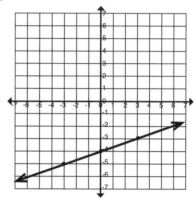

y-intercept = _____
Slope = _____
Equation of line _____

#163. Changing Equations to Slope-Intercept Form

Not all equations are written in **slope-intercept form**. You can change them to that form by isolating y on one side.

Example: $4x + 2y = 8$

Subtract 4x from both sides: $2y = 8 - 4x$

Divide both sides by 2: $\frac{2}{2}y = \frac{8}{2} - \frac{4}{2}x \longrightarrow$

$y = 4 - 2x$

Rearrange the right side: $y = -2x + 4$ (slope-intercept form)

Change each equation to slope-intercept form.

A. $2x + 3y = 9$ _____

B. $3x + y = 6$ _____

C. $-x + 2y = 4$ _____

#164. Graphing Inequalities

Graph each **inequality**. Graph the first inequality on the grid provided. Graph the rest on your own graph paper.

A. $y \leq x + 2$ B. $y > -2x - 2$

C. $y \geq \frac{1}{3}x - 1$ D. $y < x - 1$

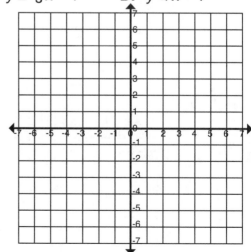

Name: _____   Date: _____

Pre-Algebra

#165. Systems of Linear Equations

Reminder: The solution of a **system of equations** (two equations written together in the same problem) is the **ordered pair** that is a solution to both equations (or where the two lines they represent cross).

Tell the ordered pair that is the solution to each system of linear equations.

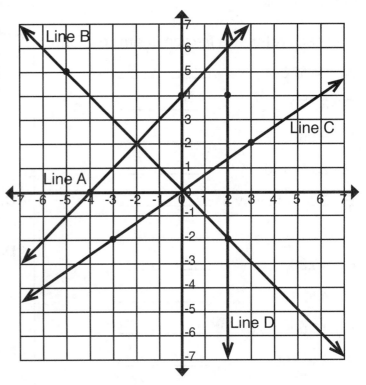

A. A and B _____

B. B and C _____

C. D and B _____

#166. Graphing Systems of Linear Equations

Find the solution to these **systems of linear equations** by graphing both equations and finding where they intersect.

A. $y = x + 3$

$y = -3x - 1$

solution: _____

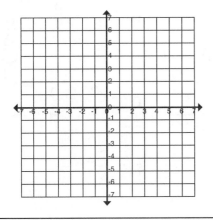

B. $y = 2x - 3$

$y = -2x + 1$

solution: _____

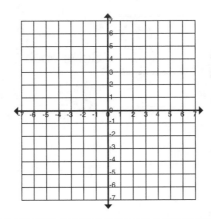

C. $y = \frac{1}{4}x + 3$

$y = 2x + 3$

solution: _____

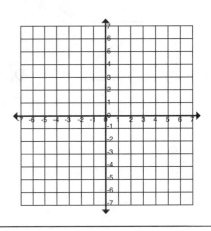

Name: _____ Date: _____

Pre-Algebra

#167. Ratios

Write each **ratio** as a fraction in simplest form.

A. 24 to 6 _____

B. 35:70 _____

C. 9 out of 27 _____

D. 25 to 100 _____

E. 2 out of every 5 _____

F. 15:33 _____

G. 45:30 _____

H. 4 to 18 _____

I. 16 out of 26 _____

J. 2 to 100 _____

#168. Rates

Express each **ratio** as a **unit rate**. For example, $6.00 for 4 pounds of oranges is $1.50/lb.

A. $20 for 5 tickets

_____

B. $42 for 14 gallons of gas

_____

C. 3.6 inches of rain in 12 hours

_____

D. $8.50 for 10 pounds of apples

_____

E. Driving 250 miles in 4 hours

_____

F. $2.16 for 4 ounces of cereal

_____

#169. Equivalent Ratios

Reminder: To find **equivalent ratios**, multiply the numerator and the denominator by the same number (except 0).

List two equivalent ratios for each ratio.

A. $\frac{3}{4}$ _____

_____

B. $\frac{1}{6}$ _____

_____

C. $\frac{10}{12}$ _____

_____

D. $\frac{4}{9}$ _____

_____

E. $\frac{9}{10}$ _____

_____

F. $\frac{2}{5}$ _____

_____

#170. Proportions

Reminder: A **proportion** is an equation that gives two equivalent ratios. The **cross products** of a proportion are always equal.

If $\frac{a}{b} = \frac{c}{d}$ then $a \cdot d = b \cdot c$.

Write *Yes* or *No* to indicate if each of these is a proportion.

A. $\frac{1}{2} = \frac{4}{8}$ _____

B. $\frac{6}{18} = \frac{3}{9}$ _____

Solve each proportion.

C. $\frac{n}{8} = \frac{6}{24}$ _____

D. $\frac{60}{15} = \frac{x}{3}$ _____

E. $\frac{16}{5} = \frac{20}{t}$ _____

F. $\frac{7}{s} = \frac{4}{8}$ _____

Name: _____ Date: _____

Pre-Algebra

#171. Changing Percents to Fractions

Reminder: To change a **percent** to a **fraction**, write it as a fraction with the denominator 100 and then simplify the fraction.

Example: $25\% = \dfrac{25}{100} = \dfrac{1}{4}$

Change each of these percents to a fraction.

A. 15% _____

B. 20% _____

C. 32% _____

D. 125% _____

E. 100% _____

F. 50% _____

G. 66% _____

H. 70% _____

I. 60% _____

#172. Changing Percents to Decimals

Reminder: To change **percents** to **decimals**, move the decimal point two places to the left and remove the percent sign.

Example: 67% = 0.67

Change each percent to a decimal.

A. 74% _____   B. 6% _____

C. 150% _____   D. 400% _____

E. 250% _____   F. 3.7% _____

G. 5% _____   H. 75% _____

I. 10% _____   J. 2.25% _____

K. 258% _____   L. 6.5% _____

#173. Changing Decimals to Percents

Reminder: To change a **decimal** to a **percent**, move the decimal point two places to the right and add the percent sign.

Examples: 0.34 = 34%   6.7 = 670%

Change each decimal to a percent.

A. 0.5 _____   B. 0.67 _____

C. 0.59 _____   D. 0.03 _____

E. 0.7 _____   F. 2.5 _____

G. 6.0 _____   H. 0.09 _____

I. 0.8 _____

DECIMALS & PERCENTS

#174. Changing Fractions to Percents

Reminder: To change a **fraction** to a **percent**, first change the fraction to an equivalent fraction with a denominator of 100. The numerator is the percent—just add the sign.

Change each fraction to a percent.

A. $\dfrac{1}{2}$ _____   B. $\dfrac{2}{5}$ _____

C. $\dfrac{1}{4}$ _____   D. $\dfrac{4}{5}$ _____

E. $\dfrac{5}{2}$ _____   F. 2 _____

G. $\dfrac{3}{4}$ _____   H. $\dfrac{6}{10}$ _____

I. $\dfrac{15}{10}$ _____

Name: _____   Date: _____

Pre-Algebra

#175. Comparing Rational Numbers

Reminder: To compare two **rational numbers**, write each so that they have the same positive denominator and then compare the numerators.

Example: $\frac{2}{3}$ ☐ $\frac{3}{4}$ → $\frac{8}{12}$ ☐ $\frac{9}{12}$.

Compare: $\frac{8}{12}$ ☐< $\frac{9}{12}$, so $\frac{2}{3}$ ☐< $\frac{3}{4}$.

Write <, >, or = in each ☐ .

A. $\frac{3}{5}$ ☐ $\frac{2}{5}$

B. $\frac{4}{8}$ ☐ $\frac{2}{4}$

C. $\frac{7}{9}$ ☐ $\frac{5}{6}$

D. $-\frac{4}{5}$ ☐ $-\frac{3}{6}$

E. $\frac{18}{6}$ ☐ $\frac{18}{9}$

F. $\frac{1}{2}$ ☐ $\frac{1}{3}$

#176. Adding Rational Numbers

Add these **rational numbers** and write in simplest form.

A. $\frac{5}{12} + \left(-\frac{5}{8}\right)$ _____

B. $\frac{3}{16} + \frac{7}{8}$ _____

C. $-\frac{1}{2} + \left(-\frac{1}{3}\right)$ _____

D. -2.6 + 4.5 _____

E. 3.9 + 6.4 _____

F. 23.7 + (-45.2) _____

G. 1.27 + 0.5 _____

H. 30.45 + (-14.3) _____

I. -9.9 + (-8.8) _____

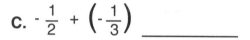

#177. Subtracting Rational Numbers

Subtract these **rational numbers** and write in simplest form.

A. $\frac{1}{4} - \frac{2}{5}$ _____

B. $4\frac{1}{2} - 7$ _____

C. $-\frac{3}{8} - \left(-\frac{1}{2}\right)$ _____

D. -6.2 – 4.1 _____

E. 55.4 – 33.6 _____

F. 121.1 – (-67.4) _____

G. 13.34 – 19.6 _____

H. -4.75 – (-3.23) _____

I. 47.5 – 45.7 _____

#178. Multiplying Rational Numbers

Multiply and write in simplest form.

A. $\frac{6}{5} \cdot \frac{5}{6}$ _____

B. $\frac{5}{6} \cdot \left(-\frac{3}{4}\right)$ _____

C. $-\frac{7}{4} \cdot \left(-\frac{7}{4}\right)$ _____

D. $2\frac{2}{3} \cdot 4$ _____

E. 1.6 · 2.4 _____

F. -2.7 · 3.1 _____

G. -7.25 · (-3.3) _____

H. 7.8 · (-5) _____

I. 4.11 · 4.2 _____

J. -6 · 5.5 _____

Name: _____ Date: _____

Pre-Algebra

#179. Dividing Rational Numbers

Divide and write in simplest form.

A. $\dfrac{3}{4} \div \dfrac{1}{2}$ _____

B. $-\dfrac{3}{4} \div \dfrac{1}{4}$ _____

C. $\dfrac{2}{3} \div \left(-\dfrac{1}{2}\right)$ _____

D. $\dfrac{5}{8} \div \dfrac{2}{3}$ _____

E. $18.4 \div 2$ _____

F. $-0.66 \div 0.3$ _____

G. $14 \div 2.2$ _____

H. $-1.8 \div (-1.2)$ _____

I. $3.25 \div 5$ _____

J. $100 \div (-0.25)$ _____

#180. Solving Equations With Rational Numbers (+/-)

Solve each equation for x.

A. $3x + 8 = 13$ _____

B. $24 - 15x = 16$ _____

C. $4x - 3 = 9$ _____

D. $-15 - 6x = 15$ _____

E. $-7x - 16 = -12$ _____

F. $18 + 12x = -6$ _____

G. $-8 - 5x = 7$ _____

H. $9 + 7x = -3$ _____

#181. Solving Equations With Rational Numbers (· / ÷)

Solve each equation for x.

A. $3.2x = 19.2$ _____

B. $\dfrac{2}{3}x = 9$ _____

C. $-5.4x = 16.2$ _____

D. $\dfrac{3}{4}x = -21$ _____

E. $\dfrac{x}{3.1} = 4$ _____

F. $\dfrac{x}{0.5} = 9$ _____

G. $\dfrac{-x}{7.25} = -2$ _____

H. $\dfrac{x}{2.2} = -2.2$ _____

#182. Solving Equations With Rational Numbers

Solve each equation for x.

A. $x - 5x = 16$ _____

B. $4x + 10x = 28$ _____

C. $8x + 6 - 5x = 6$ _____

D. $12x - x + 5 = 6$ _____

E. $7x + 4x = 33$ _____

F. $7x + 2x - 5 = 0$ _____

G. $9x - x = -48$ _____

H. $-6x + 1 - 13x = -18$ _____

Name: _____ Date: _____

Pre-Algebra

#183. Squares and Square Roots

Reminder: Every positive number has two **square roots**. One is positive and one is negative.

Example: $x^2 = 9 \longrightarrow$ 3 · 3 = 9 and
-3 · -3 = 9.
This is written as $x = \pm 3$.

Find two solutions for each equation.

A. $x^2 = 16$ _____

B. $b^2 = 25$ _____

C. $r^2 = 36$ _____

D. $d^2 = 100$ _____

E. $n^2 = 144$ _____

F. $h^2 = 64$ _____

G. $c^2 = 81$ _____

H. $t^2 = 400$ _____

#184. Square Roots

Reminder: The symbol $\sqrt{}$ is used to indicate a **nonnegative square root**, and the symbol $-\sqrt{}$, is used to indicate a **negative square root**.

Find each square root indicated.

A. $\sqrt{49}$ _____ **B.** $\sqrt{121}$ _____

C. $\sqrt{1}$ _____ **D.** $\sqrt{169}$ _____

E. $-\sqrt{4}$ _____ **F.** $-\sqrt{225}$ _____

G. $-\sqrt{100}$ _____ **H.** $-\sqrt{196}$ _____

#185. Adding and Subtracting Square Roots

Solve.

A. $\sqrt{81} - \sqrt{49}$ _____

B. $\sqrt{9} + \sqrt{16}$ _____

C. $\sqrt{121} - \sqrt{4}$ _____

D. $\sqrt{20 + 5}$ _____

E. $\sqrt{36} + \sqrt{64} + \sqrt{1}$ _____

F. $\sqrt{164 - 20}$ _____

G. $\sqrt{90 - 9} + \sqrt{54 - 5}$ _____

H. $\sqrt{9 + 7} - \sqrt{9 - 5}$ _____

#186. Multiplying and Dividing Square Roots

Solve.

A. $5 \cdot \sqrt{25}$ _____

B. $36 \div \sqrt{16}$ _____

C. $\sqrt{100} \cdot \sqrt{49}$ _____

D. $\sqrt{4 \cdot 16}$ _____

E. $\sqrt{144} \div \sqrt{4}$ _____

F. $\sqrt{9} \cdot \sqrt{4} \cdot \sqrt{49}$ _____

G. $(\sqrt{64} \cdot \sqrt{16}) \div \sqrt{4}$ _____

H. $\sqrt{25} \cdot (-\sqrt{121})$ _____

Name: _____ Date: _____

Pre-Algebra

#187. Square Roots and Rational Numbers

Reminder: To find the **square root** of a fraction, find the square root of the numerator and the square root of the denominator and simplify if necessary.

Solve.

A. $\sqrt{\dfrac{9}{16}}$ _____

B. $\sqrt{\dfrac{64}{16}}$ _____

C. $-\sqrt{\dfrac{4}{36}}$ _____

D. $\sqrt{\dfrac{49}{81}}$ _____

E. $\sqrt{\dfrac{144}{121}}$ _____

F. $-\sqrt{\dfrac{25}{100}}$ _____

G. $-\sqrt{\dfrac{169}{225}}$ _____

H. $\sqrt{\dfrac{36}{144}}$ _____

#188. Square Roots and Equations

Reminder: To solve equations with **squared variables**, isolate the squared variable and use the **square root** to solve for its root.

Example: $y^2 + 3 = 28$

Subtract 3 from both sides to get $y^2 = 25$, then take the square root of both sides.

$\sqrt{y^2} = \sqrt{25} \rightarrow y = 5$

Find the positive solution to each equation.

A. $c^2 - 6 = 30$ _____

B. $m^2 + 7 = 56$ _____

C. $a^2 - 2 = 14$ _____

D. $z^2 + 4 = 68$ _____

E. $b^2 + 9 = 90$ _____

F. $h^2 - 10 = 90$ _____

#189. The Pythagorean Theorem

The **Pythagorean Theorem** is $a^2 + b^2 = c^2$ (where a and b are the lengths of the two legs of a right triangle and c is the length of the hypotenuse of a right triangle). If you know the lengths of two of the sides, you can plug them into the formula and solve for the unknown side.

Find the length of the unknown side of each right triangle below.

A. _____
$a = 3$ $c = ?$ $b = 4$

B. _____
$c = 13$ $a = 5$ $b = ?$

C. _____
$c = 20$ $b = ?$ $a = 12$

#190. Using the Pythagorean Theorem

Use the **Pythagorean Theorem** ($a^2 + b^2 = c^2$) to help you solve each of these problems. Use a calculator and round to the nearest tenth.

A. A 10-foot tree casts a shadow 12 feet long on the ground. How far would it be from the top of the tree to the tip of its shadow?

_____

B. A TV has a diagonal of 25 inches. It is 15 inches tall. How wide is it?

_____

C. A square has sides 6 inches long. How long is its diagonal?

_____

Name: _____ Date: _____

Pre-Algebra

#191. Polynomials

Tell whether each **polynomial** is a **monomial**, a **binomial**, or a **trinomial**.

A. $6m + 2n$ _____

B. $8h^2$ _____

C. $b^2 + 3b + 4$ _____

D. $xy^2 + 2x + 4$ _____

E. $4g$ _____

F. $8t^2 - 5$ _____

G. $j^2 - 3j - 4$ _____

H. cd _____

I. $w - 5$ _____

J. $r^2 + 6r - 7$ _____

#192. Evaluating Polynomials

Evaluate each **polynomial** for $x = 1$, $y = 2$, and $z = -2$

A. $x^2 + y$ _____

B. $y^2 + z$ _____

C. $3xy$ _____

D. $x^2 + z^2$ _____

E. $2x + 2y + z$ _____

F. xyz _____

G. $x + 3y + 4z$ _____

H. $y^2 + z^2 - x$ _____

#193. Combining Like Terms in Polynomials

Reminder: A **coefficient** is the numerical part of a **monomial**. Like terms are either the same or only differ in coefficients. ***Example:*** In $3xy$, the coefficient is 3.

Give the coefficients of a and b in each expression.

A. $2a + 4b$ _____ _____

B. $-10a + b$ _____ _____

Simplify by combining like terms.

C. $2x + 4y + 3x + 7y$ _____

D. $n - 2m + 5n + 3m$ _____

E. $4r^2 + r + 3r - 2r^2 + 1$ _____

F. $6c^2d - 5cd + 4cd - 3c^2d$

_____

#194. Adding Polynomials

To add **polynomials**, combine all of the like terms from each **addend** into one polynomial.

Add.

A. $(3c + 3) + (-6c + 8)$

_____

B. $(6r + 5s + 7t) + (5r + 2t)$

_____

C. $(9a^2 - b) + (2a^2 - 2b)$

_____

D. $(3x^2 + 2x) + (4x^2 - 3x)$

_____

E. $(3x^2 + 3x) + (2x^2 + 4x)$

_____

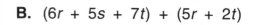

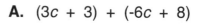
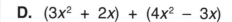

Name: _____ Date: _____

Pre-Algebra

#195. Problem Solving With Addition of Polynomials

Add **polynomials** to find the **perimeter** of each figure.

A. $2x + 5$ _____

$2x + 5$ [square] $2x + 5$

$2x + 5$

B.   _____

$4n + 2$ [triangle] $4n + 2$

$4n + 2$

C. $4c + 6$ _____

$3c + 1$ [rectangle] $3c + 1$

$4c + 6$

#196. Subtracting Polynomials

To subtract a **polynomial**, add the opposite of the polynomial.

Subtract.

A. $(3g^2 + 5g) - (g^2 + 2g)$

_____

B. $(5x + 3y) - (3x + 2y)$

_____

C. $(2b^2 + 4b) - (b^2 + 2b)$

_____

D. $(3w + 5v) - (4w + 5v)$

_____

E. $(2r^2 - 3s) - (r^2 - 4s)$

_____

#197. Multiplying Monomials

To multiply **monomials**, first multiply the **coefficients**. To multiply the **variables**, add their **exponents**.

Multiply.

A. $a^2 \cdot a^5$

_____

B. $3(4t)$

_____

C. $(3x)(2x)$

_____

D. $(-4)(3b)$

_____

E. $(2m^2)(-3n)$

_____

F. $(-3g)(2g^3)(4g^2)$

_____

G. $(-3s)(-3s)(-3s)$

_____

H. $(k^4)(2k^2)(-3k)$

_____

#198. Powers of Monomials

To find the **power of a power**, multiply the **exponents**.

Simplify.

A. $(2^2)^2$

_____

B. $(-4x^3)^2$

_____

C. $(-5bc)^3$

_____

D. $(r^3)^{-2}$

_____

E. $(fg^2)^6$

_____

F. $(y^3z)^2$

_____

G. $(j^5)^3$

_____

H. $(a^2b^2c^2)^3$

_____

Name: _____ Date: _____

Pre-Algebra

#199. Multiplying Polynomials by Monomials

Use the **distributive property** to help you multiply a **polynomial** by a **monomial**.

Example: $2x(x + 2) \longrightarrow 2x(x) + 2x(2)$
$\longrightarrow 2x^2 + 4x$

Multiply.

A. $5(n + 4)$ _____ **B.** $3a(a + 5)$ _____

C. $5t(t + 3)$ _____ **D.** $3b(b + 2)$ _____

E. $2m(3n + p)$ _____ **F.** $3x(6x + 2y)$ _____

G. $3r(2r + 3s + 4t)$ _____

#200. Evaluating Products of Polynomials and Monomials

Evaluate each expression for $x = 2$, $y = 3$.

A. $2(x + 4)$ _____ **B.** $3(y + 2)$ _____

C. $3(x + y)$ _____ **D.** $x(x + 3)$ _____

E. $2x(x + y)$ _____ **F.** $x(x + y)$ _____

G. $2y(2x - 2y)$ _____ **H.** $3x(2 + 4y)$ _____

#201. Dividing Polynomials by Monomials

To divide a **polynomial** by a **monomial**, divide each term of the polynomial by the monomial.

Example: $\dfrac{12x + 4}{4} \longrightarrow \dfrac{12x}{4} + \dfrac{4}{4} \longrightarrow 3x + 1$

Divide.

A. $\dfrac{18n^2 + 6}{6}$ _____

B. $\dfrac{8b + 2}{2}$ _____

C. $\dfrac{21t^2 + 7t}{7t}$ _____

D. $\dfrac{m^2 + m}{m}$ _____

E. $\dfrac{20a^2 + 10a}{5a}$ _____

F. $\dfrac{y^3 + y^2}{y}$ _____

#202. Multiplying Binomials

To multiply two **binomials**, multiply each term of the first binomial by each term of the second binomial using the **distributive property**.

Example: $(x + 3)(x + 4)$
$x(x + 4) + 3(x + 4)$
$x^2 + 4x + 3x + 12$
$x^2 + 7x + 12$

Multiply.

A. $(n + 4)(n + 5)$ _____

B. $(3b - 4)(2b - 6)$ _____

C. $(4t + 1)(t - 5)$ _____

D. $(x - 9)(x - 9)$ _____

BINOMIALS

Name: _____   Date: _____

Pre-Algebra

#203. Describing Patterns and Sequences

Decide which algebraic equation describes each **sequence**. Then find the next term in the sequence.

a. $x^2 - x$ **b.** $2x + 1$ **c.** $x(x + 1)$
d. $3x - 1$ **e.** x^2

A. _____   3, 7, 15, 31,... _____

B. _____   5, 14, 41, 122,... _____

C. _____   2, 4, 16, 256,... _____

D. _____   2; 6; 42; 1,806;... _____

E. _____   3, 6, 30, 870,... _____

#204. The Counting Principle

Find the number of **possible outcomes** for each situation.

A. There are 3 flavors of ice cream and 2 types of cones. How many types of one-dip ice cream cones are there to choose?

_____

B. A shirt comes in short or long sleeves, 3 different colors, and 2 different types of fabric. How many possible combinations for the shirt are there?

_____

D. You can buy a car in 6 different exterior colors, 3 different interior colors, and either manual or automatic shift. How many different choices would you have?

_____

#205. Factorials

Find the value of each **factorial**.
For example $4! = 4 \cdot 3 \cdot 2 \cdot 1 = 24$.

A. 7!   _____

B. 10!   _____

C. $\dfrac{10!}{8!}$ _____

D. $\dfrac{12!}{6!}$ _____

E. $9! - 5!$ _____

F. $2! \cdot 2!$ _____

G. $\dfrac{5!3!}{3!4!}$ _____

H. $\dfrac{7!2!}{2!5!}$ _____

#206. Probability

Reminder: To find the **probability** of a particular event occurring, write the ratio of the number of ways the event can occur over the number of possible outcomes.

Example: The probability of rolling a 2 on a die is $\frac{1}{6}$ because there is only one way to roll a 2, and there are 6 possible outcomes when you roll a die.

If you roll a die one time, what is the probability that you will roll ...

A. The number 5   _____

B. An even number   _____

C. A number less than 5   _____

D. A prime number   _____

E. A 1 or a 3   _____

Name: _____ Date: _____

Pre-Algebra

#207. Independent and Dependent Events

Reminder: Two events are **independent** if the outcome of one does not affect the outcome of the other. They are **dependent** if the outcome of one does affect the outcome of the other.

Write *I* if the event is independent and *D* if it is dependent.

A. ___ Picking a card from a deck, not replacing it, and then picking another card.

B. ___ Eating an item from a tray of snacks, then choosing another item.

C. ___ Rolling a die, and then rolling it again.

D. ___ Choosing a hat from a rack of hats, then choosing a pair of shoes from a rack of shoes.

E. ___ Choosing a marble from a bag, replacing it, and then choosing another marble.

#208. Computing the Probabilities of Two or More Independent Events

Reminder: To compute the **probability** of two or more **independent events**, multiply the probability of the first event by the probability of the second event.

Calculate each probability for having a green die and a blue die. Put answers in simplest form.

A. green 3 and blue 6

_____

B. green even and blue even

_____

C. green even and blue odd

_____

D. green 1 and blue odd

_____

E. green factor of 6 and blue factor of 12

_____

#209. Odds

Reminder: To find the **odds** in favor of an event occurring, write the **ratio** of the number of ways the event can occur to the number of ways that the event cannot occur. Simplify.

Example: What are the odds of choosing a black marble from a bag of 3 black marbles, 12 white marbles, and 5 red marbles? There are 3 chances of choosing a black and 17 chances of getting something other than a black. Write the ratio as $\frac{3}{17}$. The odds are 3 to 17 of getting a black marble.

A gumball machine has 50 red balls, 40 blue balls, 35 yellow balls, and 25 white balls. Calculate the odds in favor of getting ...

A. A blue gumball

_____

B. A red or yellow gumball

_____

C. A color other than red

_____

D. A blue or white gumball

_____

E. A color from the U.S. flag

_____

F. A color other than yellow or white

_____

Name: _____ Date: _____

Pre-Algebra

#210. Using a Sample to Make Predictions

Round answers to the nearest whole number.

A. In a sample, 20 out of 60 people said their favorite color was red. Based on the sample, how many people out of 900 would you predict like red the best? _____

B. In a sample, 25 out of 50 children said they prefer cheese pizza to pepperoni. Based on the sample, how many children out of 300 would you predict prefer cheese pizza to pepperoni? _____

C. In a sample, 22 out of 30 people said that vanilla was their favorite flavor of ice cream. Based on the sample, how many people out of 100 would you predict like vanilla ice cream the best? _____

D. In a sample, 24 out of 30 people say they have taken the bus in the past month. Based on the sample, how many people out of 200 would you predict have taken the bus in the past month? _____

#211. Using a Sample to Make Decisions

A company makes basketballs. A worker inspects the balls before they are shipped. He inspects 600 balls and finds that 12 of them are defective. He talks to the manager, and they decide to change the speed at which the balls are glued. After the change, the worker inspects 1,000 balls and 15 are defective.

A. What percent of the balls were defective before the change? _____

B. What percent are defective after the change? _____

C. Did the change help improve the process? _____

 D. If the company makes 8,000 balls per week, how many would you expect to be defective per week (after the change)? _____

Name: _____   Date: _____

Algebra

#212. Real Numbers: Order of Operations

Number these rules to show the **order of operations**.

_____ Evaluate expressions with exponents.

_____ Do all additions and subtractions in order from left to right.

_____ Do all operations within parentheses.

_____ Do all multiplications and divisions in order from left to right.

#213. Real Numbers 1

Simplify.

A. $18 - 3 \cdot 4 + 6 \div 3$

_____

B. $3(2 + 5) - 2^2$

_____

C. $4(6 + 8 - 3 + 1)$

_____

#214. Real Numbers 2

Simplify.

A. $\{20 - [3(1 + 3)]\} \cdot 2$

_____

B. $3^3 + (14 - 8) \cdot 2$

_____

C. $(4^2 + 2^2) \div 5$

_____

#215. Algebraic Expressions With One Variable

Evaluate each expression if $n = 12$.

A. $n + 15$ _____

B. $50 - n$ _____

C. $7n$ _____

D. $\dfrac{n}{4}$ _____

Name: _____ Date: _____

Algebra

#216. Algebraic Expressions With Multiple Variables

Evaluate each expression if $a = 3$, $b = 5$, and $c = 2$.

A. $3abc$ _____

B. $\frac{1}{2}a + b$ _____

C. b^c _____

#217. Algebraic Expressions With Fractions as Variables

Evaluate each expression if $p = \frac{1}{4}$ and $r = \frac{1}{2}$.

A. $p + r$ _____

B. $r - p$ _____

C. pr _____

D. $\dfrac{p}{r}$ _____

#218. Writing Algebraic Expressions 1

Write an algebraic expression that could answer each question if n is Dan's age now.

A. What was Dan's age 3 years ago?

_____

B. What age will Dan be in 8 years?

_____

C. How many years until Dan is 50?

_____

#219. Writing Algebraic Expressions 2

Write an algebraic expression for each phrase.

A. Some number n increased by 8

_____

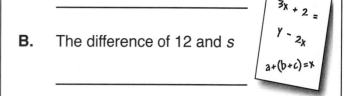

B. The difference of 12 and s

_____

C. Three less than 4 times a number t

_____

D. g divided by h

_____

Name: _____   Date: _____

Algebra

#220. Algebraic Expressions With Exponents

Evaluate each expression
if $x = 2$ and $y = 3$.

A. $x^2 y$ _____

B. $x^3 y^2$ _____

C. $x^2 + y^2$ _____

D. $-(xy)^2$ _____

#221. Evaluating Algebraic Expressions 1

Evaluate each expression.

A. x^4 if $x = 2$ _____

B. r^3 if $r = 3$ _____

C. m^3 if $m = -1$ _____

D. $n^2 - n$ if $n = 4$ _____

#222. Evaluating Algebraic Expressions 2

Evaluate each expression if $a = 3$, $b = 4$, and $c = -2$.

A. $-b + c^2$ _____

B. $(c - a)^2$ _____

C. $a^2(b + c)^2$ _____

D. $-(3a + 2c)^3$ _____

#223. Evaluating Algebraic Expressions 3

Evaluate each expression if $x = 2$ and $y = -3$.

A. $x^2 + y^2 + 1$ _____

B. $2x^2 - 3x + 5$ _____

C. $3x^2 + 2y$ _____

D. $x^3 - 2y$ _____

Name: _____   Date: _____

Algebra

#224. Algebraic Expressions With Replacement Sets

Find the **solution set** of each sentence. The **replacement set** is {-1, 0, 1}.

A. $k + 3 = 3$ _____

B. $m + 1 = 0$ _____

C. $y + 1 \leq 1$ _____

D. $2n > 2$ _____

#225. Algebraic Expressions Math Stories

A. A stereo costs $110. John paid $35 down and made 5 equal payments on the stereo. Write an algebraic equation that could be used to find out how much his payments were.

_____

B. Andrea's new coat costs $25 more than twice as much as her old one. The new coat costs $105. Write an algebraic equation that could be used to determine how much her old coat cost.

_____

#226. Operations for Linear Equations

Tell which **operation** you would perform on each side of the equation to get x alone on one side.

A. $x + 3 = 7$ _____

B. $-4 = -1 + x$ _____

C. $x - 6 = 10$ _____

D. $x - (-12) = 15$ _____

#227. Solving Linear Equations 1

Solve.

A. $a - 4 = 24$ _____

B. $m + 3 = 18$ _____

C. $r + 11 = 22$ _____

D. $12 + s = -10$ _____

Name: _____ Date: _____

Algebra

#228. Solving Linear Equations 2

Solve.

A. $b - (-4) = 10$ _____

B. $-3.4 + r = -9.5$ _____

C. $5 = x + 2\frac{1}{3}$ _____

D. $b - 3.12 = 5.23$ _____

#229. Solving Linear Equations 3

Solve.

A. $-5t = 30$ _____

B. $2x = 14$ _____

C. $\frac{x}{7} = -4$ _____

D. $\frac{3}{5}p = 12$ _____

#230. Solving Linear Equations 4

Solve.

A. $1.25x = 5$ _____

B. $\frac{2}{3}a = 4$ _____

C. $\frac{s}{5} = 10$ _____

D. $-3.5b = 14$ _____

#231. Linear Equations in Word Sentences

Write an algebraic equation for each word sentence and then solve.

A. The quotient of 30 and a number n equals 6.

_____

B. The product of 9 and a number c equals 27.

_____

Name: _____ Date: _____

Algebra

#232. Linear Equations and the Area of a Triangle

The formula to find the **area of a triangle** is $A = \frac{1}{2}bh$.

A. What is the area (A) if $b = 6$ and $h = 5$?

_____

B. What is the height (h) if $b = 4$ and $A = 16$?

_____

C. What is the base (b) if $h = 4$ and $A = 12$?

_____

#233. Linear Equations and the Circumference of a Circle

Solve. The **circumference of a circle** can be found with the formula $C = 2\pi r$.

A. Find C if $\pi = 3.14$ and $r = 10$.

_____

B. Find r if $C = 94.2$ and $\pi = 3.14$.

_____

#234. Linear Equations and the Distributive Property

Use the **distributive property** to find each product.

A. $6(n - 4)$ _____

B. $(5 + d)3$ _____

C. $25(4 + 3s)$ _____

D. $3(a + b)$ _____

#235. Solving Linear Equations 5

Solve.

A. $a + (a + 4) + (2a - 3) = 13$

_____

B. $2(y - 3) = 12$

_____

C. $8(m - 1) = 8$

_____

D. $-2(4x - 3) = -14$

_____

Name: _____   Date: _____

Algebra

#236. Inequalities and Solution Sets

Solve and state the **solution set**.

A. $|2a + 7| = 9$ _____

B. $|\frac{1}{3}b - 2| = 4$ _____

C. $|y - 4| > 6$ _____

D. $|2g - 9| \geq 1$ _____

#237. Inequalities and Graphs

Circle the sentence that best describes the graph.

A. $x \geq -2$ **B.** $x = -2$

C. $x < -2$ **D.** $x > -2$

E. $x \leq -2$

#238. Solving Inequalities 1

Solve.

A. $4y + 6 < 2y - 6$

_____

B. $5x + 2 - 4x \geq 3$

_____

C. $8c < 56$

_____

D. $\frac{3}{4}b \geq -18$

_____

#239. Solving Inequalities 2

Solve.

A. $3(m - 1) - 4 \leq 2 - 4(2 - m)$

_____

B. $-3 + 2r \neq 9 - 2r$

_____

C. $\frac{2}{3}b < -8$

_____

D. $-2.5x \leq 12.5$

_____

Name: _____ Date: _____

Algebra

#240. Rewriting Polynomials in Scientific Notation

Rewrite each number in **scientific notation**.

A. 645 _____

B. 0.0023 _____

C. 48726.5 _____

D. $(3 \cdot 10^4)\ (4 \cdot 10^5)$

_____

#241. Simplifying Polynomials in Fractional Form

Simplify. Assume that no variable equals 0.

A. $\dfrac{d^7}{d^4}$ _____

B. $\dfrac{c^2}{c^5}$ _____

C. $\dfrac{2ab^7}{5a^4}$ _____

D. $\dfrac{4x^2y^5}{2x^6y^2}$ _____

#242. Simplifying Polynomials 1

Simplify. Assume that no variable equals 0.

A. $(w^5)^6$ _____

B. $\left(\dfrac{-r}{s^3}\right)^8$ _____

C. $\left(\dfrac{4x}{5y}\right)^2$ _____

D. $\left(\dfrac{4u^2v}{-3u^5v^2}\right)^2$ _____

#243. Simplifying Polynomials 2

Simplify.

A. $(b^6)(b^3)$ _____

B. $(2n^2m)(4n^4m^3)$ _____

C. $(6x^3y)(3x^4y^4)$ _____

D. $(3a^{2x})(a^{3x})$ _____

Name: _____ Date: _____

Algebra

#244. Degrees in Polynomials

State the **degree** in each **polynomial**.

A. $3n$ _____

B. $4x^2 - 2x + 6$ _____

C. $-10ab^3c^5$ _____

D. $5u^2v^2 + 8u^2v^2 + 3uv - 2$

_____

#245. Monomials in Factored Forms

Write each **monomial** in **factored** form.

A. $-2b^3$ _____

B. $3^2x^5y^2$ _____

C. $-4a^2b^3$ _____

D. $(-x)^4$ _____

#246. Rewriting Polynomials

Rewrite each **polynomial** in descending order of the exponents with respect to x.

A. $2x - 5x^3 + 7 - x^4$

_____

B. $4x^3y^2 - x^8 + 2 - 3x^6y$

_____

C. $-6 + 8x^3y^4 - 3x^2y - 2x^5y^5$

_____

#247. Solving Polynomials

Solve.

A. $(3x^2 - 4x + 6) + (2x - 2x^2 + 2)$

_____

B. $(2m^3 - 4m^2 + m - 6) + (2m^2 + 6m^3 + 9)$

_____

Name: _____   Date: _____

Algebra

#248. Adding Polynomials

Add these **polynomials**.

A. $(3x^3 + 2x^2 - 4x - 8) + (x^2 - 3x + 9)$

_____

B. $(3a^2 - 6a - 4) + (a^2 + 9 - 7a^3 + 2a)$

_____

#249. Subtracting Polynomials

Subtract.

A. $(7e^3 - 3e^2 + 9e + 1) - (3e^3 - e^2 + 5e - 7)$

_____

B. $(6b^3 + 3b^2 - b - 6) - (b^2 - 8b + 9)$

_____

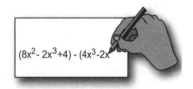

#250. Adding and Subtracting Polynomials

Add or subtract as indicated.

A. $(6x + 5y - 3z) - (4x - 3y + 2z)$

_____

B. $(3a + 2b + 4) + (7a - b + 3)$

_____

#251. Multiplying Polynomials 1

Multiply.

A. $(-4b^4)(5b^5)$

_____

B. $3x^2y(4x + 2y - r)$

_____

C. $7m^2(m^3 - 3m^4 + 5m^2)$

_____

Name: _____ Date: _____

Algebra

#252. Multiplying Polynomials 2

Multiply.

A. $(x + 5)(x - 8)$

_____

B. $(3a - 2)(5 + 6a)$

_____

C. $(2p - 3r)(4p + r)$

_____

#253. Dividing Polynomials 1

Divide.

A. $(16r^2 - 8r + 12) \div 4$

_____

B. $(12a^4 - 6a^2 + 4a) \div 2a$

_____

C. $(20n^5 + 10n^3 - 15n^2 + 5n) \div 5n$

_____

#254. Dividing Polynomials 2

Divide.

A. $(2c^2 - 3c - 2) \div (c - 2)$

_____

B. $(2y^2 + 3y - 20) \div (y + 4)$

_____

C. $(6x^2 - x - 12) \div (2x - 3)$

_____

#255. Factoring: Products

Write each as the product of its **factors** by using **exponents**.

A. $2 \cdot 2 \cdot 2 \cdot 2$ _____

B. $3 \cdot 3 \cdot 5 \cdot 5 \cdot 5$ _____

C. $2 \cdot 5 \cdot 3 \cdot 3 \cdot 3$ _____

D. $11 \cdot 11 \cdot 11 \cdot 11 \cdot 11 \cdot 13 \cdot 13$

_____

Name: _____   Date: _____

Algebra

#256. Prime Factorization

Write the **prime factorization** of each number. Use **exponents** for repeated factors.

A.   70   _____

B.   135   _____

C.   338   _____

D.   1,000   _____

#257. Factoring 1

Factor.

A. $3p + 15$ _____

B. $2r + 7r^2$ _____

C. $16x + 12y$ _____

D. $4b^2 - 8b$ _____

#258. Factoring 2

Factor.

A. $2m^3n - 12m^2n^4$

_____

B. $5x^2y - 15x^3y^3$

_____

C. $4g^2h + 8g^2h^2 + 12gh$

_____

#259. Factoring 3

Factor.

A. $9a^2b^4 - 54a^5b^3$

_____

B. $2x^3 - 6x^2 + 10x$

_____

C. $-15c^3d^4 - 35c^4d^5 - 55c^2d^4$

_____

FACTORS

Name: _____ Date: _____

Algebra

#260. Factoring 4

Factor.

A. $y^2 + 4y + 3$

_____

B. $7 + 8j + j^2$

_____

C. $k^2 + 14k + 13$

_____

D. $s^2 - 12s + 35$

_____

#261. Solving Factoring Problems

Solve.

A. $x^2 + 12x + 11$ _____

B. $48 + 19c + c^2$ _____

C. $m^2 - 9m + 14$ _____

D. $b^2 - 18b + 32$ _____

#262. Factoring by Grouping

Factor by grouping.

A. $15x^2 + 12x + 6x^3$

_____

B. $5(y - 3) + 2(y - 3) - 3(y - 3)$

_____

C. $21a - 21b + 15a - 15b$

_____

D. $mr + nr + ms + ns$

_____

#263. Solving by Factoring 2

Solve by factoring.

A. $a^2 - 8a + 15 = 0$

_____

B. $r^2 - 3r - 18 = 0$

_____

C. $2b^2 + 13b - 24 = 0$

_____

70

Name: _____   Date: _____

Algebra

#264. Simplifying Rational Expressions 1

Simplify and state the values for which the expression is **undefined**.

A. $\dfrac{3a}{12a^2}$ _____

B. $\dfrac{7x - 14}{x - 2}$ _____

C. $\dfrac{r + 2}{5r^2 + 7r - 6}$ _____

D. $\dfrac{24y + 18}{36}$ _____

#265. Simplifying Rational Expressions 2

Simplify and state the values for which the expression is **undefined**.

A. $\dfrac{2y^2 + 9y - 5}{y^2 + 10y + 25}$

_____

B. $\dfrac{9 + 11z + 2z^2}{z^2 - 10z - 11}$

_____

#266. Multiplying Rational Expressions 1

Multiply. Assume all denominators do not equal 0.

A. $\dfrac{5s}{3s^2} \cdot \dfrac{4}{s^2 y}$

_____

B. $\dfrac{12xy^2}{5y^3 z^2} \cdot \dfrac{5xz}{3x}$

_____

C. $\dfrac{2n + 4}{3n - 9} \cdot \dfrac{6n - 18}{4n + 20}$

_____

#267. Multiplying Rational Expressions 2

Multiply. Assume all denominators do not equal 0.

A. $\dfrac{h - 5}{4h + 6} \cdot \dfrac{6h + 9}{3h - 15}$

_____

B. $\dfrac{2y + 4}{6y - 8} \cdot \dfrac{y - 5}{y + 2}$

_____

C. $\dfrac{3b - 15}{4b - 2} \cdot \dfrac{20b - 10}{15b - 75}$

_____

Name: _____ Date: _____

Algebra

#268. Dividing Rational Expressions 1

Divide.

A. $\dfrac{2}{x} \div \dfrac{3y}{2x}$ _____

B. $\dfrac{a}{b} \div \dfrac{b^2}{a^3}$ _____

C. $\dfrac{9}{n} \div \dfrac{3r}{4n}$ _____

#269. Dividing Rational Expressions 2

Divide.

A. $\dfrac{2x^2}{y^2} \div \dfrac{14x}{3y}$ _____

B. $\dfrac{c + 5}{c + 14} \div (c + 5)$

_____

C. $\dfrac{s^2 - 9}{s^2 - 2s - 24} \div \dfrac{s - 3}{s - 6}$

_____

#270. Rational Expressions and Least Common Denominators

Find the **least common denominator**.

A. $\dfrac{-3}{2a^3b}$ and $\dfrac{4a}{6a^3b^5}$

_____

B. $\dfrac{5}{12x^3y}$ and $\dfrac{-3}{10xy^2}$

_____

#271. Equivalent Rational Expressions

Find the **least common denominator** and write the equivalent expressions with the LCD as denominator.

$$\dfrac{5}{9x^2y} \quad \text{and} \quad \dfrac{2x}{3y^2}$$

A. LCD _____

B. Equivalent expressions

_____

Name: _____   Date: _____

Algebra

#272. Adding and Subtracting Rational Expressions 1

Add or subtract.

A. $\dfrac{9}{2b} + \dfrac{3}{2b}$ _____

B. $\dfrac{2p}{p + 1} + \dfrac{5p}{p + 1}$ _____

C. $\dfrac{5x}{x + 2} - \dfrac{x - 8}{x + 2}$ _____

#273. Adding and Subtracting Rational Expressions 2

Add or subtract.

A. $\dfrac{5b + 1}{25 - b^2} + \dfrac{5}{b + 5}$ _____

B. $\dfrac{3}{2c} + \dfrac{2}{4c^2} - \dfrac{1}{c}$ _____

C. $\dfrac{4}{2y + 8} - \dfrac{y}{5y + 20}$ _____

#274. Simplifying Rational Expressions 1

Simplify.

A. $2 + \dfrac{1}{e}$ _____

B. $5 - \dfrac{7}{y}$ _____

C. $3i - \dfrac{i + 1}{i}$ _____

#275. Simplifying Rational Expressions 2

Simplify.

A. $\dfrac{2a - 1}{a + 2} + a$

_____

B. $\dfrac{\dfrac{k}{2} - \dfrac{k}{3}}{\dfrac{k}{6} + \dfrac{2}{3}}$

_____

Algebra

#276. Ratios in Rational Expressions

Are these **ratios** equal?

A. $\dfrac{2}{5} = \dfrac{6}{15}$ _____

B. $\dfrac{4}{8} = \dfrac{9}{15}$ _____

C. $4:5 = 8:15$ _____

D. $2:8 = 12:48$ _____

#277. Solving Ratios in Rational Expressions

Solve these **ratios**.

A. $\dfrac{5}{6} = \dfrac{30}{y}$ _____

B. $\dfrac{12d}{28} = \dfrac{15}{7}$ _____

C. $\dfrac{4}{a + 4} = \dfrac{2}{3a + 2}$

_____

#278. Rational Expressions Word Problems

A bag contains 10 red marbles, 4 green marbles, and 9 blue marbles. If you reached into the bag and took out 1 marble, what is the **probability** that ...

A. it will be red?

_____

B. it will not be red?

_____

C. it will be blue or red?

_____

#279. Linear Equations in Two Variables

Determine if each **ordered pair** is a solution of the equation: $x + 3y = 6$.

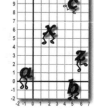

A. $(3, 1)$ _____

B. $(4, 2)$ _____

C. $(9, -1)$ _____

D. $(0, 2)$ _____

E. $(-2, 2)$ _____

Name: _____   Date: _____

Algebra

#280. Points in Linear Equations With Two Variables

Name the point that is the **graph** of each **ordered pair**.

A. (-3, -4) _____   **B.** (2, -3) _____

C. (2, 2) _____   **D.** (-1, 1) _____

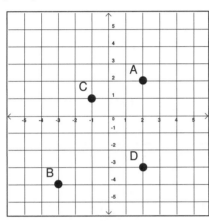

#281. Graphing Linear Equations in Two Variables

Graph the **ordered pairs** and connect the points.

A. (1, 0)   **B.** (3, 2)   **C.** (-2, 3)

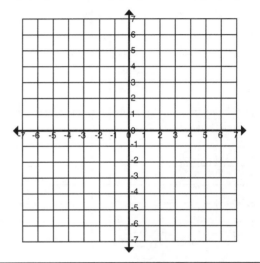

#282. Linear Equations and Solution Tables

Make a **solution table** for the equation. Then graph the following equation.

$$y = 9 - 3x$$

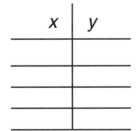

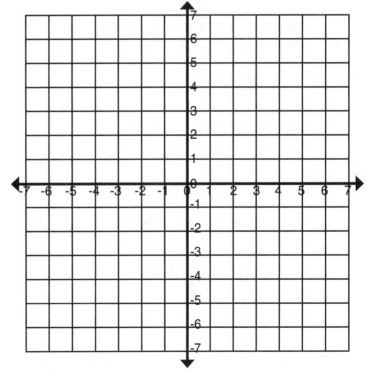

Name: _____ Date: _____

Algebra

#283. Graphing Linear Equations Using Three Points 3

Graph the equation $4y - x = 2$ using at least three points.

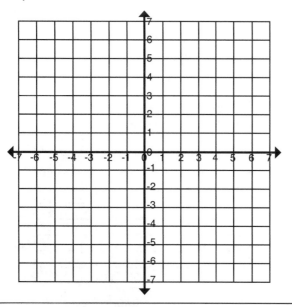

#284. Solving Linear Equations for *y*

Solve each equation for *y*.

A. $x + y = 8$

_____

B. $4x = 2y - 1$

_____

C. $3(x - 1) - 4(y + 5) = 12$

_____

#285. Linear Equations and Slope 1

Find the **slope** of a line that contains the given points.

A. A (-2, 3) B (2, 1)

_____

B. C (6, 7) D (1, 3)

_____

C. E (-1, 3) F (2, 4)

_____

#286. Linear Equations and Slope 2

Find the value of the missing **coordinate** using the given **slope**.

A (*x*, 0) and B (3, 4), slope = 2

_____

Name: _____   Date: _____

Algebra

#287. Linear Equations, Slope, and the y-Intercept 1

Find the **slope** and the **y-intercept** of the line for the given equation.

$$4x + 3y = 12$$

slope _____

y-intercept _____

#288. Linear Equations, Slope, and the y-Intercept 2

Find the **slope** and the **y-intercept** of the line for the given equation.

$$8x - y = 2$$

slope _____

y-intercept _____

#289. Linear Equations and the Slope-Intercept Form

Write an equation in **slope-intercept form** that contains the given points.

A (5, 6) B (6, 9)

_____

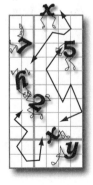

#290. Writing Linear Equations to Find Slope

Write an equation of a line in **standard form** given a point and the slope.

A.   point (0, 3)   slope: $-\frac{1}{2}$

_____

B.   point (2, 6)   slope: $\frac{3}{2}$

_____

Name: _____ Date: _____

Algebra

#291. Graphing Inequalities

Graph the **inequality** $x \geq 2$.

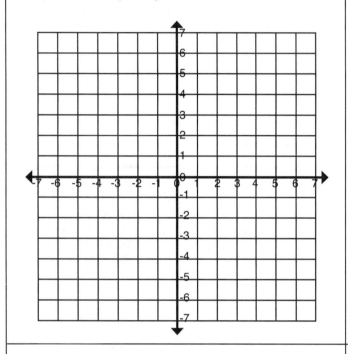

#292. Graphing Inequalities With Two Variables

Graph the **inequality** $y \geq -x + 3$.

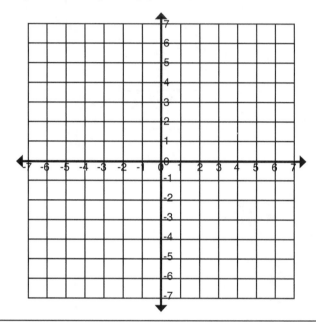

#293. Graphing Systems of Linear Equations

Solve by graphing:

$$\left\{ \begin{array}{l} x - 2y = 1 \\ x + 2y = 1 \end{array} \right\}$$

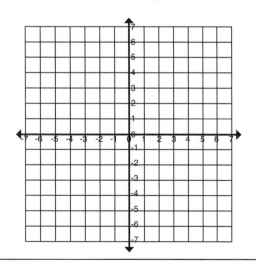

#294. Solving Systems of Linear Equations by Substitution

Solve by **substitution**.

3x - y = 17
y + 2x = 8

3x + 2y = 4
y = x - 3

7x + y = 22
5x - y = 14

A. $\left\{ \begin{array}{l} 3x + 2y = 4 \\ y = x - 3 \end{array} \right\}$

_____

B. $\left\{ \begin{array}{l} y = 3x + 1 \\ y = 6x - 1 \end{array} \right\}$

_____

Name: _____ Date: _____

Algebra

#295. Solving Systems of Linear Equations by Elimination

Solve by **elimination**.

A. $\begin{cases} x + y = 10 \\ x - y = 12 \end{cases}$

_____

B. $\begin{cases} -x + y = 4 \\ x + y = 8 \end{cases}$

_____

#296. Systems of Linear Equations: Word Problems

Write an equation for each word sentence.

A. A number n is four more than two times a number m.

_____

B. A number a is half as much as three less than a number b.

_____

C. Six years from now, Steve will be 4 years older than twice Roy's age now.

_____

D. The amount of money in dimes is half the amount of money in quarters.

_____

#297. Finding Square Roots

Find the **square roots**.

A. $\sqrt{49}$ _____

B. $\pm\sqrt{0.81}$ _____

C. $\sqrt{\frac{1}{16}}$ _____

D. $\sqrt{900}$ _____

E. $\pm\sqrt{576}$ _____

F. $\sqrt{0.0025}$ _____

G. $-\sqrt{-(2 - 11)}$ _____

H. $-\sqrt{1.96}$ _____

#298. Simplifying Roots

Simplify.

A. $\sqrt[4]{81}$ _____

B. $\sqrt[5]{32}$ _____

C. $\sqrt[3]{64}$ _____

D. $\sqrt[3]{-125}$ _____

E. $\sqrt{72}$ _____

F. $\sqrt{108}$ _____

G. $\sqrt{44}$ _____

H. $\sqrt{90}$ _____

Name: _____ Date: _____

Algebra

#299. Evaluating Square Roots

Evaluate for the given value of the variable and then simplify, if possible.

A. $\sqrt{a - 7}$, $a = 15$ _____

B. $\sqrt{b + 3}$, $b = 25$ _____

C. $\sqrt{3c + 6}$, $c = 7$ _____

#300. Simplifying Square Roots With Real Numbers 1

Simplify. Assume all variables represent non-negative **real numbers**.

A. $\sqrt{9a^3b^4}$ _____

B. $\sqrt{\frac{50}{49}}$ _____

C. $\frac{9}{\sqrt{5}}$ _____

D. $\sqrt{\frac{25}{81}}$ _____

#301. Simplifying Square Roots With Real Numbers 2

Simplify. Assume all variables represent non-negative **real numbers**.

A. $4\sqrt{11} + 3\sqrt{11}$ _____

B. $8\sqrt{15} - 4\sqrt{15}$ _____

C. $\sqrt{6} - 4\sqrt{6}$ _____

#302. Multiplying Square Roots 1

Multiply and simplify.

A. $(\sqrt{5})(\sqrt{10})$ _____

B. $(2\sqrt{3})(-3\sqrt{2})$ _____

C. $(\sqrt{\frac{9}{2}})(\sqrt{\frac{2}{3}})$ _____

Name: _____   Date: _____

Algebra

#303. Multiplying Square Roots 2

Multiply and simplify.

A. $(\sqrt{2} + 3)(\sqrt{2} - 3)$ _____

B. $\sqrt{7}(4 + \sqrt{7})$ _____

C. $(4\sqrt{n})^2$ _____

#304. Rationalizing Square Roots and Radicals 1

Rationalize the denominator and simplify.

A. $\sqrt{\dfrac{1}{2}}$ _____

B. $\dfrac{-2\sqrt{3}}{\sqrt{5}}$ _____

C. $\dfrac{3\sqrt{2}}{4\sqrt{32}}$ _____

#305. Rationalizing Square Roots and Radicals 2

Rationalize the denominator and simplify.

A. $\dfrac{4\sqrt{3}}{2\sqrt{8}}$ _____

B. $\sqrt{\dfrac{8}{y}}$ _____

C. $\sqrt{\dfrac{24x^3}{6x}}$ _____

#306. Solving Radical Equations 1

Solve these **radical** equations.

A. $\sqrt{g} = 8$ _____

B. $\sqrt{\dfrac{b}{3}} = 2$ _____

C. $\sqrt{2y - 1} - 3 = 1$

_____

Name: _____ Date: _____

Algebra

#307. Solving Radical Equations 2

Solve these **radical** equations.

A. $\sqrt{s - 2} = 3$ _____

B. $\sqrt{\dfrac{2n}{3}} + 5 = 7$ _____

C. $\sqrt{4r^2} - 27 = r$ _____

#308. Using the Pythagorean Theorem to Find Length

Use the **Pythagorean Theorem** ($a^2 + b^2 = c^2$) to find the missing lengths.

A. $a = 5, c = 13, b = ?$

_____

B. $b = 4, c = 5, a = ?$

_____

C. $a = \sqrt{3}, b = 1, c = ?$

_____

#309. Using the Pythagorean Theorem to Find Distance

Use the **Pythagorean Theorem** ($a^2 + b^2 = c^2$) to find the distance between each pair of points.

A. R (1, 2), S (4, -2)

_____

B. B (6, 2), C (6, -8)

_____

#310. Quadratic Equations

Solve by **factoring**. Express all **radicals** in simplest form.

A. $u^2 - u - 12 = 0$

_____

B. $4a^2 - 9a = 0$

_____

C. $6b^2 = 17b - 12$

_____

Name: _____   Date: _____

Algebra

#311. Quadratic Equations and Square Roots

Solve by the **square root** method. Express all **radicals** in simplest form.

A. $r^2 = \sqrt{\dfrac{4}{25}}$ _____

B. $36b^2 = 18$ _____

C. $2r^2 = 16$ _____

#312. Completing the Square in Quadratic Equations

Solve by **completing the square**. Express all **radicals** in simplest form.

A. $a^2 - 2a - 8 = 0$

_____

B. $c^2 + 10c + 3 = 0$

_____

C. $4r^2 - 12r = -9$

_____

#313. Solving Quadratic Equations 1

Solve by using the **quadratic formula**.

A. $2a^2 - 3a - 5 = 0$ _____

B. $b^2 + 5b + 6 = 0$ _____

C. $x^2 - 3x - 10 = 0$ _____

D. $r^2 - 3r + 6 = 4$ _____

#314. Solving Quadratic Equations 2

Solve each **quadratic equation** by any appropriate method.

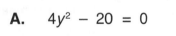

A. $4y^2 - 20 = 0$

_____

B. $s^2 - 4s = -3$

_____

Answer Keys

Teachers: Check students' work and equations if necessary.

Pre-Algebra

#001. Addition and the Value of *n* (pg. 2)
A. 11 **B.** 9 **C.** 14 **D.** 9

#002. Addition and the Value of *p* (pg. 2)
A. $18 **B.** $26 **C.** $14
D. $39

#003. Addition and the Value of *h* (pg. 2)
A. 0.44 **B.** 0.18 **C.** 0.12
D. 0.42

#004. Addition and the Value of *t* (pg. 2)
A. 8 **B.** 6 **C.** 19 **D.** 5

#005. Subtraction and the Value of *n* (pg. 3)
A. 10 **B.** 11 **C.** 46 **D.** 73

#006. Subtraction and the Value of *p* (pg. 3)
A. $52 **B.** $44 **C.** $82
D. $39

#007. Subtraction and the Value of *h* (pg. 3)
A. 1.29 **B.** 1.66 **C.** 0.28
D. 1.40

#008. Subtraction and the Value of *t* (pg. 3)
A. 2 **B.** 14 **C.** 43 **D.** 43

#009. Multiplication and the Value of *m* (pg. 4)
A. 5 **B.** 4 **C.** 7 **D.** 6

#010. Multiplication and the Value of *p* (pg. 4)
A. 4 **B.** 3 **C.** 7 **D.** 6

#011. Multiplication and the Value of *k* (pg. 4)
A. 2 **B.** 4 **C.** 3 **D.** 3

#012. Multiplication and the Value of *s* (pg. 4)
A. 10 **B.** 4 **C.** 9 **D.** 7

#013. Division and the Value of *w* (pg. 5)
A. 6 **B.** 48 **C.** 11 **D.** 35

#014. Division and the Value of *v* (pg. 5)
A. 5 **B.** $42 **C.** 9
D. $132

#015. Division and the Value of *r* (pg. 5)
A. 6 **B.** 58 **C.** 9 **D.** 64

#016. Division and the Value of *h* (pg. 5)
A. 10 **B.** 100 **C.** 1,000
D. 63,000

#017. Mixed Operations: Math Stories 1 (pg. 6)
A. She baked 23 cookies.
B. $280 **C.** $3.15

#018. Mixed Operations: Math Stories 2 (pg. 6)
A. $84 **B.** 45 carrots

#019. Writing Decimals as Fractions 1 (pg. 6)
A. $\frac{3}{4}$ **B.** $\frac{19}{20}$ **C.** $\frac{1}{5}$
D. $\frac{17}{50}$ **E.** $\frac{1}{100}$ **F.** $7\frac{7}{50}$

#020. Writing Decimals as Fractions 2 (pg. 6)
A. 0.8 **B.** 0.9 **C.** 0.07
D. 0.875 **E.** 0.5 **F.** 5.6

#021. Decimals and Fractions: Missing Numbers 1 (pg. 7)
A. $17\frac{1}{4}$ **B.** $\frac{29}{40}$ **C.** $1\frac{5}{27}$
D. $\frac{5}{14}$

#022. Decimals and Fractions: Missing Numbers 2 (pg. 7)
A. $\frac{1}{2}$ **B.** 3 **C.** 0.18
D. 5

#023. Order of Operations (pg. 7)
A. 22 **B.** 14 **C.** 15
D. 50 **E.** 31 **F.** 35
G. -25 **H.** -18

#024. Reviewing Order of Operations (pg. 7)
A. 56 **B.** 5 **C.** 24
D. -0.66 **E.** 102 **F.** 6
G. 26 **H.** 113

#025. Positive and Negative Numbers (pg. 8)
A. 11° **B.** 9° **C.** -23°
D. -46°

#026. Positive and Negative Numbers: Fill in the Blank 1 (pg. 8)
A. -3 + -1 + -5 = -9
B. (-5 × -1) + -3 = +2
C. (-5 × -3) + -1 = +14
D. (-5 + -3) ÷ -1 = +8

#027. Positive and Negative Numbers: Fill in the Blank 2 (pg. 8)
A. -5 + -6 + -7 = -18
B. (-7 × -6) + -5 = +37
C. (-5 × -6) + -7 = +23
D. (-5 × -6) ÷ -7 = -4 R2

#028. Positive and Negative Numbers: Fill in the Blank 3 (pg. 8)
A. (-6 × -5) ÷ -4 = -7 R2
B. (-4 × -6) ÷ -5 = -4 R4
C. -4 + -5 + -6 = -15
D. -6 × (-5 + -4) = +54

#029. Exponents (pg. 9)
A. 2 × 2 × 2 × 2
B. 9 × 9 × 9 × 9 × 9 × 9
C. 7 × 7 × 7
D. $y \cdot y \cdot y \cdot y \cdot y \cdot y \cdot y \cdot y \cdot y \cdot y$

#30. Exponential Expressions (pg. 9)
A. 27 **B.** 16 **C.** 32
D. 125 **E.** 3^3 **F.** 10^6
G. d^3 **H.** $m^2 + p^2$

#031. Solving for Exponents (pg. 9)
A. 16 **B.** 26 **C.** 24
D. 33 **E.** 6^2 **F.** 9^2 (or 3^4)
G. 4^2 (or 2^4) **H.** 5^2

#032. Solving Multi-Step Math Stories (pg. 9)
A. $9,600 **B.** $325
C. The youngest paid $20; the others paid $30 each.

#033. Operations Signs: <, >, = (pg. 10)
A. > **B.** < **C.** > **D.** =

#034. Operations Signs: <, >, ≤, ≥, and = (pg. 10)
A. = **B.** ≥ **C.** = **D.** >
E. ≥ **F.** < **G.** ≤

#035. Mixed Operations 1 (pg. 10)
Missing: 18

#036. Mixed Operations 2 (pg. 10)
Missing: 54

#037. Describing Number Patterns (pg. 11)
A. $31: n \times 2 + 1$ **B.** $16: n \div 2$
C. $77; 66; 55; 44: n - 11$

#038. Using Expressions to Describe Number Patterns (pg. 11)
A. n cats have 2 times n ears; $2n$
B. $3 + 2n$

#039. Drawing a Picture or Diagram (pg. 11)
A. 20 ducklings   **B.** 10 cans

#040. Drawing a Diagram (pg. 12)
A. Students should draw a 5 by 5 array of diamonds.
B. Students should continue the pattern with a triangle of 10 squares.

#041. Drawing a Picture (pg. 12)
Items drawn should show 3, 6, 9, 12, and 15 items.

#042. Using Tables to Find Patterns (pg. 12)
A. At 10 P.M., it was -11°.
B. 14 were red.

#043. Values of Variables 1 (pg. 13)
A. 52 **B.** 60 **C.** 53 **D.** 99

#044. Values of Variables 2 (pg. 13)
A. 57 **B.** 0 **C.** -13 **D.** 60

#045. Values of Variables 3 (pg. 13)
A. -40 **B.** 12 **C.** -84 **D.** -36

#046. Solving Word Problems With Values of Variables (pg. 13)
A. $b \times 0.75$ **B.** $12.75

#047. Balancing Equations With Addition (pg. 14)
A. 9 **B.** 3 **C.** $6 + 12$

#048. Balancing Equations With Subtraction (pg. 14)
A. 5 **B.** 5 **C.** $31 - 8$

#049. Balancing Equations With Multiplication (pg. 14)
A. Answer can be any number.
B. 4   **C.** $z \times 3 \times 0.5 \times 6$

#050. Balancing Equations With Division (pg. 14)
A. 7 **B.** 4 **C.** $20 \div 1$

#051. Identifying Operations to Balance Equations 1 (pg. 15)
A. subtract   **B.** subtract
C. add   **D.** add

#052. Identifying Operations to Balance Equations 2 (pg. 15)
A. multiply   **B.** divide
C. subtract   **D.** multiply

#053. Identifying Operations to Balance Equations 3 (pg. 15)
A. divide   **B.** multiply
C. add   **D.** subtract

#054. Isolating Variables to Balance Equations (pg. 15)
A. 702   **B.** 2

#055. Isolating Variables With Addition and Subtraction 1 (pg. 16)
A. 4   **B.** 74   **C.** 28

#056. Isolating Variables With Addition and Subtraction 2 (pg. 16)
A. 23   **B.** 92   **C.** 18

#057. Isolating Variables With Multiplication and Division 1 (pg. 16)
A. 3   **B.** 4   **C.** 5

#058. Isolating Variables With Multiplication and Division 2 (pg. 16)
A. 12   **B.** 21   **C.** 40

#059. Isolating Variables Mixed Practice 1 (pg. 17)
A. 3   **B.** 1   **C.** 3

#060. Isolating Variables Mixed Practice 2 (pg. 17)
A. 28   **B.** 729   **C.** 2
D. 83

#061. Isolating Variables With Order of Operations (pg. 17)
A. 4   **B.** 288   **C.** 45
D. 63

#062. Isolating Variables With Exponents (pg. 17)
A. 4   **B.** 5   **C.** 217
D. 3

#063. Isolating Variables in Math Stories (pg. 18)
A. $p \div 12 = 10; p = 120$
B. 390 inches   **C.** 39 inches

#064. Step-by-Step (pg. 18)
$n + \$1,582 = \$5,387$
$n = \$5,387 - \$1,582$
$n = \$3,805$

#065. Variables in Measurement (pg. 18)
A. $3 \times b$ or $3b$ **B.** $16 \times z$ or $16z$

#066. Variables in Distance Measurement (pg. 18)
A. $5,280 \times c$ or $5,280c$
B. $d \div 36$

#067. Variables in Liquid Measurement (pg. 19)
A. $2 \times e$ or $2e$ **B.** $f \div 4$

#068. Variables in Time Measurement 1 (pg. 19)
A. $g \times 60$ or $60g$
B. $h \times 24 \times 60$ or $1,440h$

#069. Variables in Time Measurement 2 (pg. 19)
A. $7 \times j$ or $7j$ **B.** $k \div 7$

#070. Variables in Formulas: Area of Rectangles (pg. 19)
A. $A = 5 \times 7$; 35 sq. ft.
B. $A = 9 \times 11$; 99 sq. mm

#071. Variables in Formulas: Area of Triangles (pg. 20)
A. $A = \frac{1}{2}(6)(7)$; 21 sq. ft.
B. $A = \frac{1}{2}(10)(9)$; 45 sq. in.

#072. Variables in Formulas: Volume of Rectangular Prisms (pg. 20)
A. $V = 9 \times 9 \times 9$; 729 cu. in.
B. $V = 4 \times 7 \times 8$; 224 cu. ft.
C. $V = 4 \times 8 \times 7$; 224 cu. mm

#073. Variables in Formulas: Fill in the Blanks (pg. 20)
A. area, length, width
B. The area of a triangle equals $\frac{1}{2}$ its base times its height.
C. The volume of a rectangular prism equals its length times its width times its height.

#074. Variables in Formulas: Word Problems (pg. 20)
A. 700 sq. ft.   **B.** 16 sq. in.
C. 343 cu. in.

#075. Multi-Step Operations With Variables 1 (pg. 21)
6 were 11, 15 were 12, and 9 were 13.

#076. Multi-Step Operations With Variables 2 (pg. 21)
There were 45 clownfish, 15 angelfish, 160 neon tetras, and 80 zebra fish.

#077. Multi-Step Operations With Variables 3 (pg. 21)
A. 432 trees   **B.** 144 cedar

#078. Multi-Step Operations With Variables 4 (pg. 21)
A. 6 bouquets
B. 2 more full bouquets with 2 flowers left

#079. Value of Variables Using Clues 1 (pg. 22)
The highest possible value of $b = 88$.

#080. Value of Variables Using Clues 2 (pg. 22)
The only possible value of $w = 51$.

#081. Value of Variables Using Clues 3 (pg. 22)
Students should answer two of these three possible values for n: 15; 45; 75.

#082. Value of Variables Using Clues 4 (pg. 22)
The only possible value of $c = 49$.

#083. Equations With Two Variables 1 (pg. 23)
A. $y = 35$ **B.** $y = 51$
C. $y = 7$ **D.** $y = 4$

#084. Equations With Two Variables 2 (pg. 23)
A. $g = 7\frac{1}{4}$ **B.** $g = 7$
C. $g = 2$ **D.** $g = 17\frac{1}{4}$

#085. Solving Equations With Two Variables (pg. 23)
A. 12 **B.** 2 **C.** 32 **D.** 33

#086. Writing Algebraic Expressions With Two Variables (pg. 23)
A. $r + t = 73$ or $t + r = 73$
B. $r - t = 128$ or $t - r = 128$

#087. Factors (pg. 24)
A. yes   **B.** no   **C.** no
D. yes   **E.** 2, 4   **F.** 1, 17
G. 2, 4, 8 **H.** 5, 25

#088. Divisibility (pg. 24)
A. Divisible by 2: 8, 10, 30, 36, 52, 484
B. Divisible by 3: 9, 27, 33, 24, 18, 423, 780
C. Divisible by 5: 35, 70, 90, 85, 110, 895
D. Divisible by 10: 80, 60, 20, 70, 220, 350

#089. Prime and Composite Numbers (pg. 24)
The following numbers should be circled: 2, 3, 5, 7, 11, 13, 17, 19, 23, 29, 31, 37, 41, 43, 47. The rest of the numbers should be underlined.

#090. Prime Factorization (pg. 24)
A. $2 \cdot 2 \cdot 11$ **B.** $2 \cdot 2 \cdot 2 \cdot 2 \cdot 2$
C. $3 \cdot 3 \cdot 5$ **D.** $2 \cdot 3 \cdot 3$
E. $2 \cdot 5 \cdot 5$ **F.** $2 \cdot 2 \cdot 7$

#091. Find the Greatest Common Factor (pg. 25)
A. Factors of 20: 1, 2, 4, 5, 10, 20
Factors of 36: 1, 2, 3, 4, 6, 9, 12, 18, 36
Common Factors: 1, 2, 4
GCF: 4
B. Factors of 21: 1, 3, 7, 21
Factors of 28: 1, 2, 4, 7, 14, 28
Common Factors: 1, 7
GCF: 7
C. Factors of 16; 1, 2, 4, 8, 16
Factors of 42: 1, 2, 3, 6, 7, 14, 21, 42
Common Factors: 1, 2
GCF: 2
D. Factors of 24: 1, 2, 3, 4, 6, 8, 12, 24
Factors of 48: 1, 2, 3, 4, 6, 8, 12, 16, 24, 48
Common Factors: 1, 2, 3, 4, 6, 8, 12, 24
GCF: 24

#092. Least Common Multiple (pg. 25)
A. Multiples of 4: 4, 8, 12, 16, 20, 24
Multiples of 6: 6, 12, 18, 24
LCM: 12
B. Multiples of 2: 2, 4, 6, 8, 10, 12, 14, 16, 18, 20, 22
Multiples of 7: 7, 14, 21
LCM: 14

#093. Equivalent Fractions (pg. 25)
A. 8 **B.** 6 **C.** 12 **D.** 9
E. 15 **F.** 40 **G.** 10 **H.** 35
I. 6 **J.** 8

#094. Writing Fractions in Lowest Terms (pg. 26)
A. $\frac{1}{2}$ **B.** $\frac{6}{7}$ **C.** $\frac{1}{5}$ **D.** $\frac{1}{8}$
E. $\frac{1}{3}$ **F.** $\frac{1}{9}$

#095. Adding Fractions With Like Denominators (pg. 26)
A. $\frac{5}{8}$ **B.** 1 **C.** $\frac{2}{3}$ **D.** $1\frac{1}{12}$

#096. Adding Fractions With Unlike Denominators (pg. 26)
A. $\frac{5}{6}$ **B.** $\frac{5}{8}$ **C.** $\frac{11}{15}$ **D.** $1\frac{7}{40}$
E. $\frac{11}{15}$ **F.** $\frac{3}{16}$ **G.** $\frac{8}{9}$ **H.** $\frac{3}{4}$
I. $1\frac{13}{28}$

#097. Subtracting Fractions With Like Denominators (pg. 27)
A. $\frac{1}{2}$ **B.** $\frac{2}{3}$ **C.** $\frac{2}{5}$ **D.** $\frac{1}{4}$

#098. Subtracting Fractions With Unlike Denominators (pg. 27)
A. $\frac{2}{5}$ **B.** $\frac{3}{4}$ **C.** $\frac{5}{12}$ **D.** $\frac{1}{2}$

#099. Adding and Subtracting Fractions in Word Problems (pg. 27)
A. $\frac{11}{12}$ cup   **B.** $\frac{4}{15}$

#100. Multiplying Fractions (pg. 27)
A. $\frac{3}{8}$ **B.** $\frac{1}{2}$ **C.** 1 **D.** $\frac{5}{8}$

#101. Dividing Fractions (pg. 28)
A. $1\frac{2}{3}$ **B.** 1 **C.** $\frac{9}{16}$ **D.** $\frac{5}{14}$

#102. Finding a Fraction of a Whole Number (pg. 28)
A. 4 **B.** 9 **C.** 9 **D.** 25
E. 27 **F.** 4 **G.** 19 **H.** 12

#103. Canceling in Fractions (pg. 28)
A. $\frac{1}{4}$ B. 1 C. 9 D. 1

#104. Review Adding and Subtracting Fractions/Test Taking (pg. 28)
A. b B. a C. a D. b
E. b

#105. Review Multiplying and Dividing Fractions/Test Taking (pg. 29)
A. a B. b C. a D. b
E. a

#106. Multiplying and Dividing by 10; 100; 1,000; etc. (pg. 29)
A. 13,467.99 B. 330.0085
C. 4,500 D. 2,819.19
E. 0.27007 F. 21.34599

#107. Scientific Notation (pg. 29)
A. 4 B. -3
C. $4.56 \cdot 10^8$ D. $9.46 \cdot 10^{-7}$
E. $9.3 \cdot 10^7$ F. $2.9 \cdot 10^{-3}$

#108. Adding and Subtracting Decimals (pg. 30)
A. 10.2 B. 22.41 C. 23.7
D. 31.976 E. 2.45 F. 1.94
G. 332.968 H. 1.978

#109. Multiplying Decimals (pg. 30)
A. 206.448 B. 2,390.22
C. 4.176 D. 560.32
E. 1,123.62 F. 1.984

#110. Dividing Decimals by Whole Numbers (pg. 30)
A. 1.25 B. 17.12
C. 140.616 D. 0.3447

#111. Dividing Decimals by Decimals (pg. 30)
A. 153 B. 18.5
C. 3.255 D. 8.3

#112. Review Decimals/Test Taking (pg. 31)
A. b B. a C. b D. a
E. a F. b

#113. Review +, −, x, ÷ Decimals (pg. 31)
A. 316.574 B. 964.65
C. 1,811.004 D. 61.974
E. 4.1 F. 73.0

#114. Integers and Absolute Value (pg. 31)
A. yes B. yes C. no
D. no E. -14 F. 3
G. 27 H. 42 I. 578
J. +3 K. -12 L. -7

#115. Comparing Numbers (pg. 31)
A. < B. < C. > D. >
E. = F. < G. < H. <
I. < J. <

#116. Adding Integers (pg. 32)
A. 3 B. -6 C. 34 D. 30
E. 0 F. -30 G. 49 Bonus: 1

#117. Subtracting Integers (pg. 32)
A. 3 B. 16 C. -12 D. 16
E. 12 F. -10 G. 26 H. 0
I. -20 J. 22 Bonus: 36

#118. Multiplying Integers (pg. 32)
A. 24 B. -44 C. 40 D. -42
E. 64 F. 0 G. 150
H. -21 I. -72 Bonus: 60

#119. Dividing Integers (pg. 32)
A. 6 B. -7 C. -3 D. 2
E. -3 F. 4 G. 4 H. 3
I. -12 J. 6 Bonus: -3

#120. Order of Operations (pg. 33)
A. 3 B. 8 C. 0 D. 10
E. 21 F. -19 G. 40 H. -20
Bonus: 26

#121. Evaluating Variable Expressions (pg. 33)
A. 10 B. 7 C. 6 D. 12
E. 8 F. 4 G. 4 H. 2
I. 9 J. 7 K. 31 L. 7

#122. Exponents (pg. 33)
A. 6^3 B. -5^2 C. x^5
D. $(-7)^3$ E. $11 \cdot 11$
F. $(-4)(-4)(-4)(-4)$

#123. Multiplying and Dividing Exponents (pg. 33)
A. 7^8 B. 9^4 C. r^9
D. m^5 E. 2,187 F. 7,776
G. 512 H. 343

#124. Negative Exponents (pg. 34)
A. $\frac{1}{8^2}$ B. $\frac{1}{n^{15}}$ C. $\frac{1}{5^5}$
D. $\frac{x}{y^3}$ E. 4^{-6} F. 11^{-2}
G. xy^{-5} H. mn^{-4}

#125. Order of Operations (pg. 34)
A. 15 B. 6 C. 40 D. 80
E. 9 F. -1 G. 12

#126. Properties of Numbers (pg. 34)
A. b B. d C. c D. a

#127. Commutative Property (pg. 34)
A. $7 + c = 15$ B. $d \cdot 3 = 12$
C. $m + 8 = 10$ D. $6 \cdot k = 30$
E. $11 + x = 21$ F. $4 \cdot r = 16$
G. $x + z + y = 28$, $z + x + y = 28$, $z + y + x = 28$, $x + y + z = 28$, **or** $y + z + x = 28$

#128. Associative Property (pg. 35)
A. $(45 + 55) + 38 = 138$
B. $43 + (92 + 8) = 143$
C. $(31 + 9) + (15 + 5) = 60$
D. $(4 \cdot 5) \cdot 7 = 140$
E. $48 \cdot (2 \cdot 5) = 480$
F. $(10 \cdot 10)(15 \cdot 10) = 15,000$
G. $(-2 \cdot 5) \cdot 96 = -960$

#129. Distributive Property (pg. 35)
A. $(5 \cdot 4) + (5 \cdot 5)$ B. $4w + 9w$
C. $12b + 9c$ D. $9v + 6$
E. $17g + 18$ F. $19s + 20$

#130. Properties of Zero and One (pg. 35)
A. 47 B. 65 C. 0 D. 46
E. 0 F. 32

#131. Combining Like Terms (pg. 35)
A. $5x + 3y$ B. $t + 2s$
C. $5m - 2n$ D. $5a - 4b$
E. $10c - 4d$ F. $-f + 2g$
G. $4j - 5h$ H. $10w + 7v$
I. $2y + 6z$ J. $6a + 5b + c$
K. $2h + i + 3j$ L. $3n + p$

#132. Simplifying Variable Expressions (pg. 36)
A. $4x + 12$ B. $8m - 48$
C. $6b - 3$ D. $-16n$
E. $x + 8$ F. $8c - 6$
G. $12m - 26$ H. $9g + 9h$
I. $2d + c + 7$ J. $-5x + 2y - 2$
K. $3b - 10$ L. $4a + 4b$

#133. Solving Equations by Subtracting (pg. 36)
A. $y = 3$ B. $m = 5$ C. $b = 5$ D. $z = 4$
E. $n = 14$ F. $x = 0$ G. $m = -4$ H. $z = -8$
I. $w = 0$ J. $n = -6$

#134. Solving Equations by Adding (pg. 36)
A. $b = 6$ B. $m = 11$ C. $n = 11$ D. $y = 10$
E. $a = 9$ F. $v = 4$ G. $t = 7$ H. $c = 5$
I. $m = 37$ J. $b = 1$

#135. Problem Solving With Equations (pg. 36)
A. $28 + w = 42$; $14 B. $c - 24 = 30$; 54
C. $58 + b = 80$; 22

#136. Solving Equations by Dividing (pg. 37)
A. $m = 8$ B. $t = 4$ C. $a = 9$ D. $x = 11$
E. $p = 3$ F. $z = 10$ G. $y = -7$ H. $g = 6$
I. $t = \frac{1}{3}$ J. $j = \frac{1}{4}$

#137. Solving Equations by Multiplying (pg. 37)
A. $x = 20$ B. $m = 16$ C. $g = 50$ D. $n = 0$
E. $w = 12$ F. $k = -12$ G. $h = 45$

#138. Solving Equations by Dividing or Multiplying (pg. 37)
A. $a = -15$ B. $b = 6$ C. $n = 6$ D. $w = 35$
E. $y = 36$ F. $x = 12$ G. $d = 16$

#139. Problem Solving Using Equations (pg. 37)
A. $12c = 84$; 7 B. $9b = \$4.05$; \$0.45
C. $6w = \$54$; \$9 D. $\frac{m}{8} = \$1.95$; \$15.60

#140. Solving Two-Step Equations 1 (pg. 38)
A. $x = 2$ B. $y = 3$ C. $m = 3$ D. $d = 4$
E. $h = -8$ F. $n = 6$ G. $b = 3$ H. $f = 8$
I. $a = 4$ J. $p = 3$

#141. Solving Two-Step Equations 2 (pg. 38)
A. $t = 44$ B. $b = 15$ C. $x = 8$ D. $m = 21$
E. $z = 20$ F. $w = 9$ G. $y = 90$

#142. Problem Solving by Writing and Solving Equations (pg. 38)
A. $8n + 12 = 60$; 6 B. $7n + 3 = 38$; 5
C. $5n + 10 = 55$; 9 D. $\frac{n}{4} + 7 = 15$; 32

#143. Problem Solving Using Equations/ Test Practice (pg. 38)
A. a B. a C. a

#144. Simplifying and Solving Equations 1 (pg. 39)
A. $x = 5$ B. $n = 4$ C. $b = 3$ D. $t = -2$
E. $s = 6$ F. $y = 8$ G. $t = 2$ H. $r = 7$
I. $m = 33$ J. $p = -5$

#145. Simplifying and Solving Equations 2 (pg. 39)
A. $n = 9$ B. $z = 4$ C. $t = 5$ D. $k = 3$
E. $c = 21$ F. $h = 2$ G. $g = 6$ H. $j = 4$

#146. Inequalities (pg. 39)
A. yes B. no C. no D. yes E. no
F. $x \geq 46$ G. $p \leq 200$ H. $r \geq 52$
I. $b \geq 6$ J. $c < 12$

#147. Graphing Inequalities 1 (pg. 39)
Any variables are acceptable.
A. $y < 4$ B. $n \leq 0$ C. $m \geq 2$ D. $b < 6$

#148. Graphing Inequalities 2 (pg. 40)
A.
B.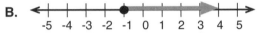
C. (line)
D. (line)

#149. Solving Inequalities by Adding and Subtracting (pg. 40)
A. $x < 2$

B. $y > 5$
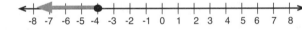
C. $a \leq -4$

D. $r < 6$

E. $s \geq -2$

#150. Solving Inequalities by Dividing or Multiplying (pg. 40)
A. $q \geq 4$
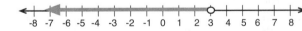
B. $n < 3$

C. $c > -1$

D. $x \leq 2$
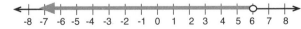
E. $s < 6$

#151. Review Solving Inequalities/ Test Taking (pg. 40)
A. b   **B.** a   **C.** a   **D.** b
E. b   **F.** a

#152. Graphing in the Coordinate Plane: Identifying Points (pg. 41)
A. K   **B.** C   **C.** M   **D.** A
E. F   **F.** L   **G.** (2, 3)
H. (6, -5)   **I.** (-5, -4)   **J.** (0, -4)
K. (-6, -3)   **L.** (-1, -1)   **M.** (5, 1)
N. (-5, 6)

#153. Graphing in the Coordinate Plane: Draw a Figure (pg. 41)

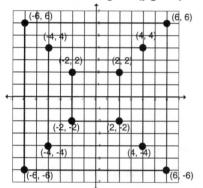

#154. Graphing Linear Equation (pg. 42)

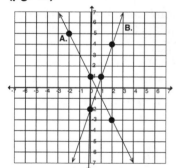

#155. Finding Slope From a Graph (pg. 42)
A. $\frac{3}{4}$ **B.** 2

#156. Slope (pg. 42)

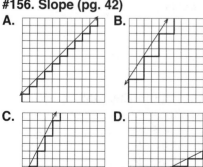

#157. Negative Slope and Zero Slope (pg. 43)
A. -2   **B.** 0

#158. Finding Slope Using Two Points (pg. 43)
A. $-\frac{1}{3}$ **B.** -3   **C.** $\frac{1}{2}$
D. $\frac{1}{3}$ **E.** 1   **F.** 1

#159. Graphing Linear Equations Using Slope (pg. 43)

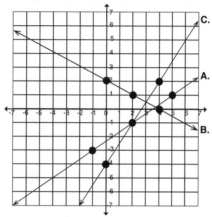

#160. Finding x- and y-Intercepts (pg. 43)
A. x-intercept: -1; y-intercept: 2
B. x-intercept: 1; y-intercept: 1
C. x-intercept: 1; y-intercept: -3

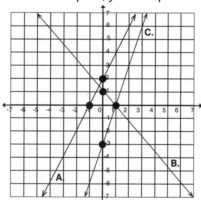

#161. Equations in Slope-Intercept Form (pg. 44)
A. slope: $\frac{1}{3}$ y-intercept: -6
B. slope: -3   y-intercept: 4
C. slope: $-\frac{2}{5}$ y-intercept: $-\frac{1}{2}$
D. slope: 4   y-intercept: -2

#162. Writing an Equation for a Line (pg. 44)
y-intercept: -4; slope: $\frac{1}{3}$;

equation: $y = \frac{1}{3}x - 4$

#163. Changing Equations to Slope-Intercept Form (pg. 44)
A. $y = -\frac{2}{3}x + 3$ **B.** $y = -3x + 6$
C. $y = \frac{1}{2}x + 2$

#164. Graphing Inequalities (pg. 44)
A.

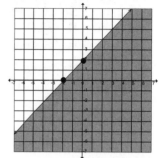

B.

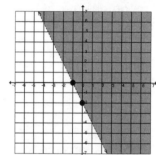

C.

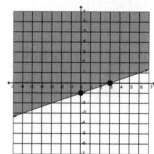

D.

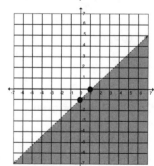

#165. Systems of Linear Equations (pg. 45)
A. (-2, 2)   **B.** (0, 0)   **C.** (2, -2)

#166. Graphing Systems of Linear Equations (pg. 45)
A. (-1, 2)   **B.** (1, -1)   **C.** (0, 3)

#167. Ratios (pg. 46)
A. $\frac{4}{1} = 4$ B. $\frac{1}{2}$ C. $\frac{1}{3}$ D. $\frac{1}{4}$
E. $\frac{2}{5}$ F. $\frac{5}{11}$ G. $\frac{3}{2}$ H. $\frac{2}{9}$
I. $\frac{8}{13}$ J. $\frac{1}{50}$

#168. Rates (pg. 46)
A. $4/ticket   B. $3/gallon
C. 0.3 inches/hr.   D. $0.85/lb
E. 62.5 mph   F. $0.54/oz.

#169. Equivalent Ratios (pg. 46)
Answers will vary—some possibilities listed here:
A. $\frac{6}{8}, \frac{12}{16}$ B. $\frac{2}{12}, \frac{3}{18}$ C. $\frac{20}{24}, \frac{50}{60}$
D. $\frac{8}{18}, \frac{12}{27}$ E. $\frac{18}{20}, \frac{27}{30}$ F. $\frac{4}{10}, \frac{6}{15}$

#170. Proportions (pg. 46)
A. yes   B. yes   C. 2
D. 12   E. 6.25   F. 14

#171. Changing Percents to Fractions (pg. 47)
A. $\frac{3}{20}$ B. $\frac{1}{5}$ C. $\frac{8}{25}$ D. $1\frac{1}{4}$
E. 1   F. $\frac{1}{2}$ G. $\frac{33}{50}$ H. $\frac{7}{10}$ I. $\frac{3}{5}$

#172. Changing Percents to Decimals (pg. 47)
A. 0.74   B. 0.06   C. 1.5
D. 4   E. 2.5   F. 0.037
G. 0.05   H. 0.75   I. 0.1
J. 0.0225 K. 2.58   L. 0.065

#173. Changing Decimals to Percents (pg. 47)
A. 50%   B. 67%   C. 59%
D. 3%   E. 70%   F. 250%
G. 600%   H. 9%   I. 80%

#174. Changing Fractions to Percents (pg. 47)
A. 50%   B. 40%   C. 25%
D. 80%   E. 250%   F. 200%
G. 75%   H. 60%   I. 150%

#175. Comparing Rational Numbers (pg. 48)
A. >   B. =   C. <   D. <
E. >   F. >

#176. Adding Rational Numbers (pg. 48)
A. $-\frac{5}{24}$ B. $1\frac{1}{16}$ C. $-\frac{5}{6}$
D. 1.9   E. 10.3   F. -21.5
G. 1.77   H. 16.15   I. -18.7

#177. Subtracting Rational Numbers (pg. 48)
A. $-\frac{3}{20}$ B. $-2\frac{1}{2}$ C. $\frac{1}{8}$
D. -10.3   E. 21.8   F. 188.5
G. -6.26   H. -1.52 I. 1.8

#178. Multiplying Rational Numbers (pg. 48)
A. 1   B. $-\frac{5}{8}$ C. $3\frac{1}{16}$
D. $10\frac{2}{3}$ E. 3.84   F. -8.37
G. 23.925   H. -39   I. 17.262
J. -33

#179. Dividing Rational Numbers (pg. 49)
A. $1\frac{1}{2}$ B. -3   C. $-1\frac{1}{3}$
D. $\frac{15}{16}$ E. 9.2   F. -2.2
G. 6.36   H. 1.5   I. 0.65
J. -400

#180. Solving Equations With Rational Numbers (+/-) (pg. 49)
A. $1\frac{2}{3}$ B. $\frac{8}{15}$ C. 3   D. -5
E. $-\frac{4}{7}$ F. -2   G. -3   H. $-1\frac{5}{7}$

#181. Solving Equations With Rational Numbers ($\cdot$ / ÷) (pg. 49)
A. 6   B. 13.5   C. -3
D. -28   E. 12.4   F. 4.5
G. 14.5   H. -4.84

#182. Solving Equations With Rational Numbers (pg. 49)
A. -4   B. 2   C. 0   D. $\frac{1}{11}$
E. 3   F. $\frac{5}{9}$ G. -6   H. 1

#183. Squares and Square Roots (pg. 50)
A. $x = \pm 4$ B. $b = \pm 5$ C. $r = \pm 6$
D. $d = \pm 10$ E. $n = \pm 12$ F. $h = \pm 8$
G. $c = \pm 9$ H. $t = \pm 20$

#184. Square Roots (pg. 50)
A. 7   B. 11   C. 1   D. 13
E. -2   F. -15 G. -10 H. -14

#185. Adding and Subtracting Square Roots (pg. 50)
A. 2   B. 7   C. 9   D. 5
E. 15   F. 12   G. 16   H. 2

#186. Multiplying and Dividing Square Roots (pg. 50)
A. 25   B. 9   C. 70   D. 8
E. 6   F. 42   G. 16   H. -55

#187. Square Roots and Rational Numbers (pg. 51)
A. $\frac{3}{4}$ B. 2   C. $-\frac{1}{3}$ D. $\frac{7}{9}$
E. $1\frac{1}{11}$ F. $-\frac{1}{2}$ G. $-\frac{13}{15}$ H. $\frac{1}{2}$

#188. Square Roots and Equations (pg. 51)
A. 6   B. 7   C. 4   D. 8
E. 9   F. 10

#189. The Pythagorean Theorem (pg. 51)
A. 5   B. 12   C. 16

#190. Using the Pythagorean Theorem (pg. 51)
A. 15.6 feet   B. 20 inches
C. 8.5 inches

#191. Polynomials (pg. 52)
A. binomial   B. mononomial
C. trinomial   D. trinomial
E. mononomial   F. binomial
G. trinomial   H. mononomial
I. binomial   J. trinomial

#192. Evaluating Polynomials (pg. 52)
A. 3   B. 2   C. 6   D. 5
E. 4   F. -4   G. -1   H. 7

#193. Combining Like Terms in Polynomials (pg. 52)
A. 2, 4   B. -10, 1
C. $5x + 11y$ D. $6n + m$
E. $2r^2 + 4r + 1$ F. $3c^2 d - cd$

#194. Adding Polynomials (pg. 52)
A. $-3c + 11$ B. $11r + 5s + 9t$
C. $11a^2 - 3b$ D. $7x^2 - x$
E. $5x^2 + 7x$

#195. Problem Solving With Addition of Polynomials (pg. 53)
A. $8x + 20$ B. $12n + 6$
C. $14c + 14$

#196. Subtracting Polynomials (pg. 53)
A. $2g^2 + 3g$ B. $2x + y$
C. $b^2 + 2b$ D. $-w$
E. $r^2 + s$

#197. Multiplying Monomials (pg. 53)
A. a^7 B. $12t$ C. $6x^2$
D. $-12b$ E. $-6m^2 n$ F. $-24g^6$
G. $-27s^3$ H. $-6k^7$

#198. Powers of Monomials (pg. 53)
A. 2^4 **B.** $16x^6$ **C.** $-125b^3c^3$
D. r^{-6} **E.** f^6g^{12} **F.** y^6z^2
G. j^{15} **H.** $a^6b^6c^6$

#199. Multiplying Polynomials by Monomials (pg. 54)
A. $5n + 20$ **B.** $3a^2 + 15a$
C. $5t^2 + 15t$ **D.** $3b^2 + 6b$
E. $6mn + 2mp$ **F.** $18x^2 + 6xy$
G. $6r^2 + 9rs + 12rt$

#200. Evaluating Products of Polynomials and Monomials (pg. 54)
A. 12 **B.** 15 **C.** 15 **D.** 10
E. 20 **F.** 10 **G.** -12 **H.** 84

#201. Dividing Polynomials by Monomials (pg. 54)
A. $3n^2 + 1$ **B.** $4b + 1$ **C.** $3t + 1$
D. $m + 1$ **E.** $4a + 2$ **F.** $y^2 + y$

#202. Multiplying Binomials (pg. 54)
A. $n^2 + 9n + 20$
B. $6b^2 - 26b + 24$
C. $4t^2 - 19t - 5$
D. $x^2 - 18x + 81$

#203. Describing Patterns and Sequences (pg. 55)
A. b; 63 **B.** d; 365
C. e; 65,536 **D.** c; 3,263,442
E. a; 756,030

#204. The Counting Principle (pg. 55)
A. 6 **B.** 12 **C.** 36

#205. Factorials (pg. 55)
A. 5,040 **B.** 3,628,800 **C.** 90
D. 665,280 **E.** 362,760
F. 4 **G.** 5 **H.** 42

#206. Probability (pg. 55)
A. $\frac{1}{6}$ **B.** $\frac{3}{6} = \frac{1}{2}$ **C.** $\frac{4}{6} = \frac{2}{3}$
D. $\frac{3}{6} = \frac{1}{2}$ **E.** $\frac{2}{6} = \frac{1}{3}$

#207. Independent and Dependent Events (pg. 56)
A. D **B.** D **C.** I **D.** I
E. I

#208. Computing the Probabilities of Two or More Independent Events (pg. 56)
A. $\frac{1}{36}$ **B.** $\frac{1}{4}$ **C.** $\frac{1}{4}$ **D.** $\frac{1}{12}$ **E.** $\frac{5}{9}$

#209. Odds (pg. 56)
A. 4 to 11 **B.** 17 to 13
C. 2 to 1 **D.** 13 to 17
E. 23 to 7 **F.** 3 to 2

#210. Using a Sample to Make Predictions (pg. 57)
A. 300 **B.** 150 **C.** 73
D. 160

#211. Using a Sample to Make Decisions (pg. 57)
A. 2% **B.** 1.5% **C.** yes
D. 120

Algebra

#212. Real Numbers: Order of Operations (pg. 58)
2, 4, 1, 3

#213. Real Numbers 1 (pg. 58)
A. 8 **B.** 17 **C.** 48

#214. Real Numbers 2 (pg. 58)
A. 16 **B.** 39 **C.** 4

#215. Algebraic Expressions With One Variable (pg. 58)
A. 27 **B.** 38 **C.** 84 **D.** 3

#216. Algebraic Expressions With Multiple Variables (pg. 59)
A. 90 **B.** 6.5 **C.** 25

#217. Algebraic Expressions With Fractions as Variables (pg. 59)
A. $\frac{3}{4}$ **B.** $\frac{1}{4}$ **C.** $\frac{1}{8}$ **D.** $\frac{1}{2}$

#218. Writing Algebraic Expressions 1 (pg. 59)
A. $n - 3$ **B.** $n + 8$ **C.** $50 - n$

#219. Writing Algebraic Expressions 2 (pg. 59)
A. $n + 8$ **B.** $12 - s$ **C.** $4t - 3$
D. $\frac{g}{h}$

#220. Algebraic Expressions With Exponents (pg. 60)
A. 12 **B.** 72 **C.** 13 **D.** -36

#221. Evaluating Algebraic Expressions 1 (pg. 60)
A. 16 **B.** 27 **C.** -1 **D.** 12

#222. Evaluating Algebraic Expressions 2 (pg. 60)
A. 0 **B.** 25 **C.** 36 **D.** -125

#223. Evaluating Algebraic Expressions 3 (pg. 60)
A. 14 **B.** 7 **C.** 6 **D.** 14

#224. Algebraic Expressions With Replacement Sets (pg. 61)
A. { 0 } **B.** { -1 } **C.** { -1, 0 }
D. { }

#225. Algebraic Expressions Math Stories (pg. 61)
A. $5n + 35 = 110$ **B.** $2x + 25 = 105$

#226. Operations for Linear Equations (pg. 61)
A. Subtract 3. **B.** Add 1.
C. Add 6. **D.** Subtract 12.

#227. Solving Linear Equations 1 (pg. 61)
A. 28 **B.** 15 **C.** 11 **D.** -22

#228. Solving Linear Equations 2 (pg. 62)
A. 6 **B.** -6.1 **C.** $2\frac{2}{3}$
D. 8.35

#229. Solving Linear Equations 3 (pg. 62)
A. -6 **B.** 7 **C.** -28 **D.** 20

#230. Solving Linear Equations 4 (pg. 62)
A. 4 **B.** 6 **C.** 50 **D.** -4

#231. Linear Equations in Word Sentences (pg. 62)
A. $30/n = 6$, $n = 5$
B. $9c = 27$, $c = 3$

#232. Linear Equations and the Area of a Triangle (pg. 63)
A. $A = 15$ **B.** $h = 8$ **C.** $b = 6$

#233. Linear Equations and the Circumference of a Circle (pg. 63)
A. $C = 62.8$ **B.** $r = 15$

#234. Linear Equations and the Distributive Property (pg. 63)
A. $6n - 24$ **B.** $15 + 3d$
C. $100 + 75s$ **D.** $3a + 3b$

#235. Solving Linear Equations 5 (pg. 63)
A. 3 **B.** 9 **C.** 2 **D.** 2.5

#236. Inequalities and Solution Sets (pg. 64)
A. {1, -8} **B.** {18 ,-6}
C. $y > 10$, $y < -2$
D. $g \leq 4$, $g \geq 5$

#237. Inequalities and Graphs (pg. 64)
A

#238. Solving Inequalities 1 (pg. 64)
A. $y < \text{-}6$ B. $x \geq 1$ C. $c < 7$
D. $b \geq \text{-}24$

#239. Solving Inequalities 2 (pg. 64)
A. $m \geq \text{-}1$ B. $r \neq 3$ C. $b < \text{-}12$
D. $x \geq \text{-}5$

#240. Rewriting Polynomials in Scientific Notation (pg. 65)
A. $6.45 \cdot 10^2$ B. $2.3 \cdot 10^{-3}$
C. $4.87265 \cdot 10^4$ D. $1.2 \cdot 10^{10}$

#241. Simplifying Polynomials in Fractional Form (pg. 65)
A. d^3 B. $\dfrac{1}{c^3}$ C. $\dfrac{2b^7}{5a^3}$
D. $\dfrac{2y^3}{x^4}$

#242. Simplifying Polynomials 1 (pg. 65)
A. w^{30} B. $\dfrac{r^8}{s^{24}}$ C. $\dfrac{16x^2}{25y^2}$
D. $\dfrac{16}{9u^6v^2}$

#243. Simplifying Polynomials 2 (pg. 65)
A. b^9 B. $8n^6m^4$ C. $18x^7y^5$
D. $3a^{5x}$

#244. Degrees in Polynomials (pg. 66)
A. 1   B. 2   C. 9   D. 4

#245. Monomials in Factored Forms (pg. 66)
A. $\text{-}2 \cdot b \cdot b \cdot b$
B. $3 \cdot 3 \cdot x \cdot x \cdot x \cdot x \cdot y \cdot y$
C. $\text{-}4 \cdot a \cdot a \cdot b \cdot b \cdot b$
D. $(\text{-}x)(\text{-}x)(\text{-}x)(\text{-}x)$

#246. Rewriting Polynomials (pg. 66)
A. $\text{-}x^4 - 5x^3 + 2x + 7$
B. $\text{-}x^8 - 3x^6y + 4x^3y^2 + 2$
C. $\text{-}2x^5y^5 + 8x^3y^4 - 3x^2y - 6$

#247. Solving Polynomials (pg. 66)
A. $x^2 - 2x + 8$
B. $8m^3 - 2m^2 + m + 3$

#248. Adding Polynomials (pg. 67)
A. $3x^3 + 3x^2 - 7x + 1$
B. $\text{-}7a^3 + 4a^2 - 4a + 5$

#249. Subtracting Polynomials (pg. 67)
A. $4e^3 - 2e^2 + 4e + 8$
B. $6b^3 + 2b^2 + 7b - 15$

#250. Adding and Subtracting Polynomials (pg. 67)
A. $2x + 8y - 5z$ B. $10a + b + 7$

#251. Multiplying Polynomials 1 (pg. 67)
A. $\text{-}20b^9$
B. $12x^3y + 6x^2y^2 - 3x^2yr$
C. $7m^5 - 21m^6 + 35m^4$

#252. Multiplying Polynomials 2 (pg. 68)
A. $x^2 - 3x - 40$
B. $18a^2 + 3a - 10$
C. $8p^2 - 10pr - 3r^2$

#253. Dividing Polynomials 1 (pg. 68)
A. $4r^2 - 2r + 3$
B. $6a^3 - 3a + 2$
C. $4n^4 + 2n^2 - 3n + 1$

#254. Dividing Polynomials 2 (pg. 68)
A. $2c + 1$ B. $2y - 5$ C. $3x + 4$

#255. Factoring: Products (pg. 68)
A. 2^4 B. $3^2 \cdot 5^3$ C. $2 \cdot 5 \cdot 3^3$
D. $11^5 \cdot 13^2$

#256. Prime Factorization (pg. 69)
A. $2 \cdot 5 \cdot 7$ B. $3^3 \cdot 5$
C. $2 \cdot 13^2$ D. $2^3 \cdot 5^3$

#257. Factoring 1 (pg. 69)
A. $3(p + 5)$ B. $r(2 + 7r)$
C. $4(4x + 3y)$ or $2(8x + 6y)$
D. $4b(b - 2)$ or $2b(2b - 4)$

#258. Factoring 2 (pg. 69)
A. $2m^2n(m - 6n^3)$
B. $5x^2y(1 - 3xy^2)$
C. $4gh(g + 2gh + 3)$

#259. Factoring 3 (pg. 69)
A. $9a^2b^3(b - 6a^3)$
B. $2x(x^2 - 3x + 5)$
C. $\text{-}5c^2d^4(3c + 7c^2d + 11)$

#260. Factoring 4 (pg. 70)
A. $(y + 1)(y + 3)$
B. $(1 + j)(7 + j)$
C. $(k + 1)(k + 13)$
D. $(s - 5)(s - 7)$

#261. Solving Factoring Problems (pg. 70)
A. $(x + 1)(x + 11)$
B. $(3 + c)(16 + c)$
C. $(m - 2)(m - 7)$
D. $(b - 2)(b - 16)$

#262. Factoring by Grouping (pg. 70)
A. $3x(5x + 4 + 2x^2)$ B. $4(y - 3)$
C. $36(a - b)$ D. $(m + n)(r + s)$

#263. Solving by Factoring (pg. 70)
A. $a = 5, 3$ B. $r = 6, \text{-}3$
C. $b = \text{-}8, \dfrac{3}{2}$

#264. Simplifying Rational Expressions 1 (pg. 71)
A. $\dfrac{1}{4a}, a \neq 0$ B. $7, x \neq 2$
C. $\dfrac{1}{5r - 3}, r \neq \dfrac{3}{5}, \text{-}2$ D. $\dfrac{4y + 3}{6}$

In D., there is no value where the expression is undefined.

#265. Simplifying Rational Expressions 2 (pg. 71)
A. $\dfrac{2y - 1}{y + 5}, y \neq \text{-}5$
B. $\dfrac{2z + 9}{z - 11}, z \neq 11$

#266. Multiplying Rational Expressions 1 (pg. 71)
A. $\dfrac{20}{3s^3y}$ B. $\dfrac{4x}{yz}$ C. $\dfrac{n + 2}{n + 5}$

#267. Multiplying Rational Expressions 2 (pg. 71)
A. $\dfrac{1}{2}$ B. $\dfrac{y - 5}{3y - 4}$ C. 1

#268. Dividing Rational Expressions 1 (pg. 72)
A. $\dfrac{4}{3y}$ B. $\dfrac{a^4}{b^3}$ C. $\dfrac{12}{r}$

#269. Dividing Rational Expressions 2 (pg. 72)
A. $\dfrac{3x}{7y}$ B. $\dfrac{1}{c + 14}$ C. $\dfrac{s + 3}{s + 4}$

#270. Rational Expressions and Least Common Denominators (pg. 72)
A. $6a^3b^5$ B. $60x^3y^2$

#271. Equivalent Rational Expressions (pg. 72)
A. $9x^2y^2$ **B.** $\dfrac{5y}{9x^2y^2}$ $\dfrac{6x^3}{9x^2y^2}$

#272. Adding and Subtracting Rational Expressions 1 (pg. 73)
A. $\dfrac{6}{b}$ **B.** $\dfrac{7p}{p+1}$ **C.** 4

#273. Adding and Subtracting Rational Expressions 2 (pg. 73)
A. $\dfrac{26}{(5-b)(b+5)}$ **B.** $\dfrac{c+1}{2c^2}$
C. $\dfrac{10-y}{5(y+4)}$

#274. Simplifying Rational Expressions 1 (pg. 73)
A. $\dfrac{2e+1}{e}$ **B.** $\dfrac{5y-7}{y}$
C. $\dfrac{3i^2-i-1}{i}$

#275. Simplifying Rational Expressions 2 (pg. 73)
A. $\dfrac{a^2+4a-1}{a+2}$ **B.** $\dfrac{k}{k+4}$

#276. Ratios in Rational Expressions (pg. 74)
A. yes **B.** no **C.** no
D. yes

#277. Solving Ratios in Rational Expressions (pg. 74)
A. 36 **B.** 5 **C.** 0

#278. Rational Expressions Word Problems (pg. 74)
A. $\frac{10}{23}$ **B.** $\frac{13}{23}$ **C.** $\frac{19}{23}$

#279. Linear Equations in Two Variables (pg. 74)
A. yes **B.** no **C.** yes
D. yes **E.** no

#280. Points in Linear Equations With Two Variables (pg. 75)
A. B **B.** D **C.** A **D.** C

#281. Graphing Linear Equations in Two Variables (pg. 75)

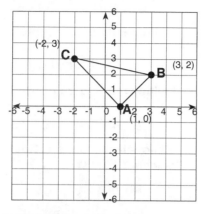

#282. Linear Equations and Solution Tables (pg. 75)
Table will vary.

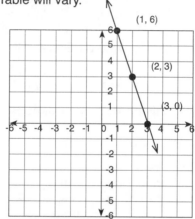

#283. Graphing Linear Equations Using Three Points 3 (pg. 76)

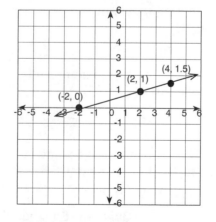

#284. Solving Linear Equations for y (pg. 76)
A. $y=8-x$ **B.** $\dfrac{y=4x+1}{2}$
C. $\dfrac{y=3x-35}{4}$

#285. Linear Equations and Slope 1 (pg. 76)
A. $-\frac{1}{2}$ **B.** $\frac{4}{5}$ **C.** $\frac{1}{3}$

#286. Linear Equations and Slope 2 (pg. 76)
$x=1$

#287. Linear Equations, Slope, and the y-Intercept 1 (pg. 77)
slope $= -\frac{4}{3}$ y-intercept $= 4$

#288. Linear Equations, Slope, and the y-Intercept 2 (pg. 77)
slope $= 8$ y-intercept $= -2$

#289. Linear Equations and the Slope-Intercept Form (pg. 77)
$y=3x-9$

#290. Writing Linear Equations to Find Slope (pg. 77)
A. $x+2y=6$ **B.** $-3x+2y=6$

#291. Graphing Inequalities (pg. 78)

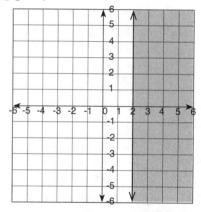

#292. Graphing Inequalities With Two Variables (pg. 78)

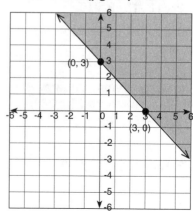

#293. Graphing Systems of Linear Equations (pg. 78)

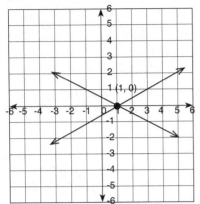

#294. Solving Systems of Linear Equations by Substitution (pg. 78)

A. (2, -1)   **B.** $(\frac{2}{3}, 3)$

#295. Solving Systems of Linear Equations by Elimination (pg. 79)
A. (11, -1)   **B.** (2, 6)

#296. Systems of Linear Equations: Word Problems (pg. 79)

A. $n = 2m + 4$ **B.** $a = \frac{1}{2}(b - 3)$
C. $S + 6 = 2R + 4$
D. $0.10d = \dfrac{0.25q}{2}$

#297. Finding Square Roots (pg. 79)

A. 7   **B.** ±0.9   **C.** $-\frac{1}{4}$
D. 30   **E.** ±24   **F.** 0.05
G. -3   **H.** -1.4

#298. Simplifying Roots (pg. 79)
A. 3   **B.** 2   **C.** 4
D. -5   **E.** $6\sqrt{2}$ **F.** $6\sqrt{3}$
G. $2\sqrt{11}$ **H.** $3\sqrt{10}$

#299. Evaluating Square Roots (pg. 80)
A. $2\sqrt{2}$ **B.** $2\sqrt{7}$ **C.** $3\sqrt{3}$

#300. Simplifying Square Roots With Real Numbers 1 (pg. 80)
A. $3ab^2\sqrt{a}$ **B.** $\dfrac{5\sqrt{2}}{7}$

C. $\dfrac{9\sqrt{5}}{5}$ **D.** $\frac{5}{9}$

#301. Simplifying Square Roots With Real Numbers 2 (pg. 80)
A. $7\sqrt{11}$ **B.** $4\sqrt{15}$ **C.** $-3\sqrt{6}$

#302. Multiplying Square Roots 1 (pg. 80)
A. $5\sqrt{2}$ **B.** $-6\sqrt{6}$ **C.** $\sqrt{3}$

#303. Multiplying Square Roots 2 (pg. 81)
A. -7   **B.** $4\sqrt{7}+7$ **C.** $16n$

#304. Rationalizing Square Roots and Radicals 1 (pg. 81)
A. $\dfrac{\sqrt{2}}{2}$ **B.** $-\frac{2}{5}\sqrt{15}$ **C.** $\frac{3}{16}$

#305. Rationalizing Square Roots and Radicals 2 (pg. 81)
A. $\dfrac{\sqrt{6}}{2}$ **B.** $\dfrac{2\sqrt{2y}}{y}$ **C.** $2x$

#306. Solving Radical Equations 1 (pg. 81)
A. 64   **B.** 12   **C.** $\frac{17}{2}$

#307. Solving Radical Equations 2 (pg. 82)
A. 11   **B.** 6   **C.** -9

#308. Using the Pythagorean Theorem to Find Length (pg. 82)
A. $b = 12$ **B.** $a = 3$ **C.** $c = 2$

#309. Using the Pythagorean Theorem to Find Distance (pg. 82)
A. 5   **B.** 10

#310. Quadratic Equations (pg. 82)
A. (4, -3)   **B.** $(0, \frac{9}{4})$ **C.** $(\frac{3}{2}, \frac{4}{3})$

#311. Quadratic Equations and Square Roots (pg. 83)

A. $\pm\dfrac{\sqrt{10}}{5}$ **B.** $\pm\dfrac{\sqrt{2}}{2}$ **C.** $\pm 2\sqrt{2}$

#312. Completing the Square in Quadratic Equations (pg. 83)
A. (-2, 4)   **B.** $-5 \pm \sqrt{22}$ **C.** $\frac{3}{2}$

#313. Solving Quadratic Equations 1 (pg. 83)
A. $(-1, \frac{5}{2})$ **B.** (-3, -2)
C. (5, -2)   **D.** (2, 1)

#314. Solving Quadratic Equations 2 (pg. 83)
A. $\pm\sqrt{5}$ **B.** (3, 1)